# MOTHERING ALONE

# MOTHERING ALONE
## A Plea for Opportunity

*Mary Kay O'Neil*

PHOENIX
PUBLISHING HOUSE
*firing the mind*

First published in 2022 by
Phoenix Publishing House Ltd
62 Bucknell Road
Bicester
Oxfordshire OX26 2DS

British Library Cataloguing in Publication Data

A C.I.P. for this book is available from the British Library

ISBN-13: 978-1-912691-31-9

Typeset by Medlar Publishing Solutions Pvt Ltd, India

www.firingthemind.com

*To my mother, Eileen,*

*who mothered three children alone*

# Contents

## Part I
## Attitudes, research, and motherhood

**Part II**
**Maternal growth**

**Part III**
**Development of mothers alone**

# Acknowledgments

The stimulus which inspired this book came about in two phases. Through the generosity and encouragement of the mothers involved in the study and numerous colleagues and friends at each phase, *Mothering Alone: A Plea for Opportunity* has come to fruition. I want to acknowledge and thank those many people whose help made this endeavor possible.

The initial phase comprised the formal research. I gratefully extend my first thank you to the Chagnon Foundation of Montreal because, without their grant, the research on which the book is based would not have been possible. It is to Dr. William Lancee, my long-time collaborator, that a most sincere thank you is due for his astute consultation on research design, data analysis, and searching questions about the meaning of the findings. Others, such as Teresa Capel (President of the Board) and current and past Executive Directors of Project Chance, assisted me in making the findings meaningful within the context and history of Project Chance. A detailed report of the research findings, "Program Outcome Study, Contributors to Mother and Child Development," was written separately for submission in English and French to Project Chance and the Chagnon Foundation (O'Neil, Capel, Hachey, 2008).

The recorded interviews kept niggling away at me. I felt the women's stories, told in their own words, had to be made known to a wider audience. It was the generosity, courage, and strength of the mothers, who told their story openly and honestly, that provided the true impetus of this book. They represent the many women mothering alone who struggle to achieve a good life for themselves and their children. As a psychologist and psychoanalyst, I also wanted to consider in writing what these women could teach about women's psychic development. Again, Bill Lancee provided stimulus: "Tell their story!" The acceptance of Phoenix to publish, assisted by their motto "Firing the Mind" and the persistent, gentle encouragement of Kate Pearce, continued to fire my mind. This motto stayed with me through the uncertainty of deciding from hundreds of transcribed pages which quotes best represented the women's situations and which stories best portrayed the lives of mothers alone with different degrees of vulnerabilities.

My thanks go to the insightful publisher Kate, to the astute editor James Darley, and the designer of the expressive cover, as well as to others at Phoenix who contributed but whose names are unknown to me. Dr. Rosemary Balsam, who has written in depth about women's development, wrote a lovely foreword, for which I am grateful. Dr. Salman Akhtar, my loyal and congenial co-editor on many books, not only introduced me to Phoenix but also gave continual encouragement and the opportunity to first present my work at the Margaret S. Mahler Symposium in Philadelphia (O'Neil, 2016). Many other colleagues and friends, Drs. Maxine Anderson, George Boujoff, Christine Dunbar, and Dorothy Markiewicz, as well as my sister, my brother, and their partners listened to my ideas and struggles, giving their time and patience to keep me persistent. To them, to my endorsers and others whom I may have missed, I express much heartfelt appreciation.

My deepest appreciation goes to my dear husband, Dr. Frederick Lowy, and to my adult children and their families. Fred was unstinting with his loving patience, reading and rereading, correcting and editing. My children and their families, with their "keep going mom and grandma," were always there. Thank you to my significant people.

# About the author

**Mary Kay O'Neil**, PhD, is a supervising and training psychoanalyst and registered psychologist in private practice in Toronto, Ontario, Canada. Trained at the Toronto Institute of Psychoanalysis, she received her PhD from the University of Toronto and was an assistant professor in the Department of Psychiatry. Currently, she is president of the North American Psychoanalytic Confederation (NAPsaC), a member of the board of the Toronto Psychoanalytic Society, and on the faculty of the Toronto Institute. Formerly, she served as director of the Canadian Institute of Psychoanalysis (Quebec English), Montreal, and was a North American representative on the board of the International Psychoanalytical Association (IPA). In addition, she was a member of a number of IPA committees, including ethics and publications and also on the editorial board of the *International Journal of Psychoanalysis*. Author of *The Unsung Psychoanalyst: The Quiet Influence of Ruth Easser*, she co-edited seven other books and has contributed numerous journal articles as well as chapters and book reviews. Her research includes studies of depression, young adult development, sole-support mothers, the analyst as art collector, post-termination contact, and psychoanalytic ethics. Toronto and Montreal Foundations have funded her research activities.

# Foreword

Mary Kay O'Neil, from Toronto, Canada, brings her many years of expertise as a sensitive, knowledgeable, and compassionate psychologist and psychoanalyst, to the study of what it is like to "mother alone." Hers is a felicitous phrase. It is much more emotionally apt than the common term "single mothers." That descriptor touches on how society unfairly disrespects such women because they are not coupled with men, and therefore are objects of suspicion—as if they somehow had engaged in foolish, deviant, and even immoral behavior, and now they deserved to face punishing consequences, such as in the stories of unwed mothers who were forced to give up their babies. O'Neil notes all this unfortunate history. She puts the emotional accent in the right place. Being solo in life, with one or more children as dependents, is a hard, uphill, lonely and exhausting—if also a potentially rewarding—task. How can such a woman find time or opportunity for further education? If she does not, though, her earning power will be automatically diminished, and she can all too easily fall afoul of the cycle of poverty many solo mothers face.

Hence, in Montreal, Canada, the sensible and humanitarian connection of such mothers to "Project Chance," a program which supports post-secondary education, and the emotional welfare and safety of these "sole-support" mothers. Dr. O'Neil was invited to study the efficacy of this program from 2006–2009. The qualitative research of recorded interviews is what inspires her present book.

The author has long nurtured in her professional work a special fascination with how women grow and develop. She signals that reading about women's lives also expands her repertoire, and she uses examples of mothers, from novels, a memoir, and a movie. O'Neil's female developmental theme has emerged from time to time, in amongst her long record of co-editing with Salman Akhtar many scholarly books about general psychoanalytic theory, under the auspices of the International Psychoanalytical Association. In addition, she has done yeoman work organizationally to support psychoanalysis, as well as carrying on her private practice and teaching; in short, she herself is a working, caretaking mother of four and of our field.

Her present book brings us back in time to her wonderful first and solo authored book about her personal analyst, Dr. Ruth Easser. Perhaps it is only my fantasy, but I think O'Neil's first love is her profound interest in women's lives, to which, later in her career, she now returns. She described the book on Ruth Easser as a part of mourning her lost analyst, to whom she was very admiringly attached. She had had only a few short years in analysis, cut short by Ruth's unexpected death. The book, published in 2004, was also about experiences from the 1970s and before. O'Neil's analyst bucked the trend of that earlier era's presentation of psychoanalysis as an "objective" one-person science, turning towards the impact of the interpersonal connections. Her biographer analysand too was free to be "contemporary" in her interactive, intersubjective attitudes. She thus, for example, did not try to conceal her writing as a mourning process. Nor did she distance herself from it. She demonstrated a sublimation of her psychic work of internalization of this beloved mother-professional, even as she investigated her life and connections. She unfolded aspects of psychoanalysis's evolution there as well.

This was an immersive participation in psychoanalysis as a "two-person" process, rather than the older, chillier, passing ideal of "one-person" systems. The latter I would take further as exemplary of the intellectual ideals of the phallocentrism that dominated a psychoanalytic theory of "normality," but that merely mirrored and mirrors society's trends of misogyny and denigration of females. Female psychology certainly suffered from exceptionally distorted and stunted development in that era, up till about the 1980s. Dr. Easser's main focus may not have been on females per se, and she did not write much, but O'Neil noted her panel contributions within national meetings, and her awareness of females qua female, there. Her study of Easser spoke poignantly to what life was like for a female analyst, in the more male professional world back then, and her struggles, joys, and tragedies.

Jumping to the present, Dr. O'Neil dedicates this book to her own mother, whom we learn was widowed at twenty-seven, a "mother alone" bringing up three children under three years old. Her father, posted to Europe when her mother was eight months pregnant, was killed in World War II six months later, and she stalwartly garnered more secondary education while looking after her growing little ones. She went to work as a teacher and librarian to support her family. So, the subtle threads of Mary Kay O'Neil's autobiography are woven into these research textures and writing. And we are grateful for it, recognizing these days—along with my own last guru, Hans Loewald—incidentally also the child of a lone mother due to a father's death—that the stuff of revisiting past experiences and deeply transforming them renders sublimation the very lifeblood of vitality for the psyche.

Dr. O'Neil has extremely interesting things to say about her lone mothers and lone parents. Her writing is a model of clarity and she is a pleasure to read. Back in 2004 she noted that "For Easser, empathy is not an echoing, but a resonance which does not distort, constrict, infantilize, or provoke emotional flight." O'Neil's whole emotional and intellectual grasp of growing womanhood, I believe, is imbued with this rich gift and brought to bear on her study. She tells her subjects' stories eloquently, with her deep grasp of their strengths and dilemmas. The reader will discover in these pages the differences "Project Chance" made to them and their families. Hidden in here—offered effortlessly and organic to the text—is a lovely, fulsome, modern account of psychoanalytic ideas about female development, and the conditions for optimal and suboptimal emotional growth. I will not act as a "spoiler." A reader will gain a lot of intimate knowledge from these marvelous case reports and commentaries, as well as the dynamic theory that accompanies her thinking at all times.

Mental health workers, including psychotherapists and psychoanalysts, and child educators should read this book, and policy-makers too should pay close attention. Mary Kay O'Neil's solo mothers are shown to sustain a powerful family force field of life that warrants great investment for the welfare of our future generations.

*Rosemary H. Balsam, FRCPsych (London), MRCP (Edinburgh)*
*Associate clinical professor of psychiatry, Yale Medical School*
*Staff psychiatrist, Yale Student Mental Health and Counseling*
*Training and supervising analyst, Western New England*
*Institute for Psychoanalysis*
*Winner of the Sigourney Award for excellence in the*
*Advancement of Psychoanalysis*

# Introduction

The seeds for this book were planted in a study I undertook in 2006 to 2009 into sole-support mothers in Canada involved in a program to facilitate their post-secondary education. The program, "Project Chance," focused on providing the opportunity for women mothering alone to have post-secondary education which would not have been available to them otherwise. The purpose of the study was to evaluate the program's efficacy and I was asked to be the principal investigator. I felt the study opened up a fascinating and underexplored window on the position and needs of women alone with children in contemporary society. Thinking about my mother's story (Appendix I) and being a child raised by a single parent provided further motivation for my interest in writing about women mothering alone.

Single motherhood is, of course, not a new phenomenon. However, in the last few decades with the evolving recognition of women's rights it is a newly accepted kind of mothering. Mothering alone is not restricted to single women; many married women find themselves in the position of having to mother children on their own. Husbands and fathers can be absent due to abandonment, divorce, death, or resulting from father-debilitating circumstances such as accidents, war, emigration, and, more frequently now, migration. Since the two world wars of the twentieth century, more women are in the workforce and able to earn their own money. Despite this societal acceptance of women working, it remains difficult to balance motherhood and work, especially without sufficient education, finances or resources, and assistance from a partner, parents, or others outside the immediate family. Parenthood—having and raising a child—is a life's work which invokes intense ambivalent feelings—love, devotion, frustration, competitiveness, humor, even tragedy. Yet, sole-support mothers, whether single or alone through other circumstances, have an even more daunting task in contemporary society. Statistics worldwide show that women mothering alone are on the increase, and they all face similar challenges. Frequently they are a vulnerable, disadvantaged, and poverty prone group who present a widespread societal problem. Many single mothers come from families with long-standing dependence on the welfare system and often exhibit a high degree of social and emotional problems. Without adequate opportunity and support, an inter-generational cycle of dependence can persist with negligible opportunity for improvement in family life.

A brief note on my definition of motherhood seems warranted: "Motherhood" is not necessarily gender related—men can "mother" and women can "father." In other words, both genders can fulfill either parenting role when necessary or by choice. A man can be left to parent alone through choice or circumstance. Men may be in similar situations as women parenting alone, and as such some aspects of this book may be relevant for them, but men parenting alone also face different challenges which are not discussed here. The same can be said of people in same gender relationships, of those identifying as non-binary or those who choose to change their birth gender. These parents too can face challenges similar to and different from those discussed here. Indeed, for anyone, parenthood is a challenging role.

Adrienne Harris (2008) suggests that, as our understanding of gender evolves, the functions of parenting can be performed by all genders. In support of this notion, she states: "As functions like containment, authorizing sexuality, paving a way to separation and autonomy, cultivating dependency and regression get dislocated from gender, become more gender agnostic, many other features of character and subjectivity may carry these psychic and intersubjective functions; generational differences, rather than more strictly gender differences, may be more prominent" (pp. 54, 55). However, only a biological female can become pregnant and give birth; only a woman, once pregnant, can choose to carry her pregnancy to full term. Once she has a child, a woman can now have the option of deciding whether or not to mother alone. Furthermore, a woman mothering alone most often has to be both father and mother.

As well as examples from my research of women mothering alone, I have brought in stories from fiction, memoirs, biographies, and clinical examples from my own practice. The women in the study who were hampered by limited resources are contrasted with examples from literature of women facing various challenges in different decades but with sufficient internal and external resources to raise their children alone. A person's capacity to adapt includes all aspects of their physical, psychological, and socio/cultural conditions,  and therefore, biopsychosocial factors as well as practical needs and self-development wishes must be taken into account.

I also focus on the psychological understanding of women related to the developmental implications of giving birth and of a woman's decision to take responsibility to raise her child(ren) on her own. Theories of women's development have been drawn primarily from psychotherapeutic case examples and rarely include contributions from the life experiences of other women mothering alone. I am convinced that much can be learned about a woman's psychological development from examples of how sole-support mothers manage their own and their children's lives despite difficult, even traumatic life experiences.

Women with few resources who mother alone are the primary focus here; the texture and relevance of their parenting situation are provided by their backgrounds and relationships, their social conditions, their current circumstances, their problems, needs, and opportunities to improve their own and their children's lives. The UNICEF report (2006) in "The Year of the Woman" affirmed the need for such a focus: "The lives of women are inextricably linked to the well-being of children. If they are not educated, if they are not healthy, if they are not empowered, the children are the ones who suffer."

This book considers what can be learned about women's development from the women in my study who, in their own words, described their early and current life experiences. It is divided into three parts:

Part I—Societal attitudes, research, and motherhood—comprises six chapters: Chapter 1 considers the societal and attitudinal changes towards single motherhood which have occurred over time, especially in the twentieth and twenty-first centuries. Chapter 2 describes the relevance of my study to the focus of the book. Research findings are in Appendix II. Chapter 3 focuses on the maternal tasks involved in raising a child. Chapter 4 touches on the women's experience of becoming mothers as well as the various influences on their decision to give birth and mother alone. Chapter 5 describes the women's own parental and relational experiences with their partners, the fathers of their children, and with others. Chapter 6 further portrays how these women develop through examples of their life stories.

Part II—Maternal growth—addresses resilience (Chapter 7), autonomy (Chapter 8), and caring (Chapter 9). I consider these three characteristics basic to effective mothering.

Part III—Development of mothers alone—considers what has been learned in the light of current psychological understanding (Chapter 10), and Chapter 11 outlines society's role in providing, for women mothering alone, the opportunity to become successful mothers.

The Afterword (Chapter 12) offers the reader a summary of what was learned through the generosity, openness, and sincerity of the women on whose contributions much of this book is based. Although improvements in societal attitudes and opportunities for women on their own with children have occurred over the years, much more needs to change. I hope to underline, as well, the need for further improvements and increased opportunity. This book, therefore, is about the status, the role, the development, and the challenges of women with few resources who mother alone in the Western world, what they need to succeed, what they contribute to the understanding of the development of women in general, and the necessity for further societal changes and opportunity. As a psychoanalyst, I also consider what these women contribute to the understanding of women's development within psychoanalytic theory.

# Part I

## Attitudes, research, and motherhood

## CHAPTER 1

# Attitudinal changes

## Women and motherhood

Women and motherhood have been linked inextricably since the beginning of time. Until recently, a woman was not free to choose to be a mother. If married, motherhood was often inevitable; unmarried women, if pregnant, had little choice. The married woman's "wifely duty" was to bear children; pregnancy and mothering were destiny. Wives in many situations had little control over the number of children they bore, especially for those who did not believe in or have access to family planning, contraception, or abortion. Indeed, for a married woman to remain child-free (regardless of the reason or her feelings) was considered at least suspect and at most reprehensible.

On the other hand, society offered unmarried women scant opportunity to mother an "out of wedlock" child. Indeed, words such as "out of wedlock," "illegitimate," and "bastard" accused both the woman and her child. Nathaniel Hawthorne's *The Scarlet Letter* (1850) portrays well the early North American shame and punishment of a woman (Hester Prynne) bearing a child outside marriage as well as the ostracization of her child (Pearl).

> She [Hester] remembered—betwixt a smile and a shudder—the talk of the neighbouring townspeople; who, seeking vainly else-where for the child's paternity, and observing some of her odd attributes, had given out that poor little Pearl was a demon off-spring; such as, ever since old Catholic times, had occasionally been seen on earth, through the agency of their mothers' sin, and to promote some foul and wicked purpose. (Chap. 6, p. 98)

Such condemnation remained well into the twentieth century and rem-nants still linger today.

## History of attitudinal change

Previously, not only was there general societal disapproval, but even within the mental health field there was a judgmental, pathologizing attitude toward single motherhood. Leontine Young's 1954 book *Out of Wedlock* is one example of a beginning attitudinal shift, as Robert Fliess notes in his foreword, from "the nineteenth century where it [unwed motherhood] had to be judged, into the twentieth where it has to be understood" (p. v). The young women[1] in her study were consid-ered, within the social context, "illegitimately pregnant" and shameful because of their obvious sexual activity. Young, however, questioned: "Why does a girl become an unmarried mother?" (p. 21). With more empathy than was previously socially and professionally common, she made a somewhat less judgmental attempt to understand the meaning of an unmarried woman bearing a child. She suggested that only a few out-of-wedlock pregnancies occur through ignorance or irresponsibility while, for the majority, the action is often subconscious and originates in the woman's family background.

Pathology was seen to lie in that

> the woman's urge for a baby has been separated from its normal matrix, love for a mate. ... The "normal" woman does not have to

---

[1] Young's theoretical understanding was psychoanalytic and her study of the unmarried mother and her child was based on more than 1,000 cases from social workers, includ-ing her own.

have a baby regardless of cost to herself or others, and she knows she wants a baby. Furthermore, she also wants the child which that baby will become and she wants to share the happiness and the responsibility of the rearing of that child with her husband. None of this is true for the unmarried mother. She must have the baby no matter what this means for herself or for others, but she is completely unconscious that this is so. (p. 37)

Young attempted to integrate the girls' life experiences with her own observations to identify the problems faced by women with "illegitimate" children. Even into the latter half of the twentieth century, it was presumed that pregnancy indicated marriage. The everyday phrase "unwed mother" shifted to the less pejorative "single mother" in the 1960s, but a wedding and stay-at-home motherhood were still held out as the family norm. Up until the late 1960s and even into the early 1970s, there was little if any socially acceptable opportunity for a young unmarried woman to keep and raise her baby. Being pregnant "out of wedlock" brought "shame" not only to the young girls or women but also to their families. To alleviate this shame, a pregnant, unmarried girl, when loose clothes no longer hid her pregnancy, would be sent in secret to a home for unwed mothers and a story would be concocted for her absence—that she had been ill, was visiting, was needed by a distant family member, or had a faraway summer job. The girl would stay at the home until she gave birth.[2] The shame also extended to her baby who would be given up for adoption because keeping an "illegitimate" child was unacceptable. The baby's birth mother would then return home without her baby as though nothing had happened. No attention was given to the psychological implications of giving birth and then placing her child for adoption.

---

[2] More recently, public attention has been given to the situations which the pregnant women faced in the homes for unwed mothers. In many, the women were treated as servants or inmates in workhouses and often abused, if not physically, at least emotionally, due to a condemning attitude—what these fallen women had done was shameful and deserved punishment. Even in the homes where they were well cared for, the attitude that their pregnancy was shameful prevailed (see, e.g., Goulding, J., *The Light in the Window*; National Institute of Social Work: Mother and Baby Homes; Petrie, A., *Gone to an Aunt's*).

Ann Fessler, in her book *The Girls Who Went Away* (2006), documented the history of multiple women who were forced to bear and then give up their children for adoption due to enormous family and societal pressure in the decades prior to the 1973 United States Supreme Court decision in Roe vs. Wade. Fessler, who had been adopted into a loving family and knew she was adopted, wrote, "I had never heard the story of adoption from the perspective of a mother who had surrendered her child." Her book underlines the pain of those involved—the birth mother and father (if he knew), the adoptive parents, and the adopted child.

At the time, there was a double standard. It was the woman's fault for becoming pregnant out of wedlock and the shame rested with her. The man remained blameless.[3]

> The girls who went away were told by family members, social-service agencies and clergy that relinquishing their child for adoption was the only acceptable option. It would preserve their reputation and save both mother and child from a lifetime of shame. Often it was clear to everyone, except the expectant mother, that adoption was the answer. (Fessler, 2006, p. 9)

The blame and guilt on the birth side of the adoption rested with the mother who gave up her baby.

Furthermore, infertility or inability to bear children was usually thought to be the fault of the woman. Consequently, for many decades child-free couples would adopt in secret to spare the married woman's embarrassment at not bearing her own child. Gradually, especially after World War II, the absence of children and adoption became more socially accepted. "Families who wanted to adopt were carefully screened and represented a kind of model family—one with a mother and a father who really *wanted* to raise a child" (Fessler, 2006, p. 2).

Concomitantly, as adoption became more acceptable, the children were told that they were adopted and that they were wanted. Often the adoptive parents were good parents and it seems that family problems were no more or less prevalent than in birth families. However, just as

---

[3] See Pfuhl (1978).

children who have lost a parent through death wonder what that parent was like and what the course of life would have been had the parent lived, adopted children also wonder about their birth parents. Yet there is a difference; at least since the early 2000s, when adoption records were opened so that the adopted child's birth mother (and sometimes father) can be searched for, with varying outcomes. Negatively, fear, regret, disappointment, rejection, anger, hurt; positively, new information with regard to identity, physical characteristics, genetic traits and illnesses; additional parental relationships, new support, pride, gratefulness—all are possible outcomes of the searching experience. The wish to search touches everyone involved—the adoptive parents, the child, the woman who relinquished her baby, and the birth father (if known). Adoptive parents can understand and support their child's wish to meet a birth parent or they can be resentful. A child can be afraid or relieved to meet a birth parent and vice versa. At times, the meeting is joyful and results in satisfactory relationships all round; other times, either the child or birth parent refuse to meet, and hopes for a relationship are damaged, or one or both parties for personal reasons wish to maintain secrecy.

Fessler gives firsthand accounts of the excruciating pain of separation endured by these "unwed" women who had been pressured to give up their children. The stories on which Fessler bases her book are shocking when considering the enormous pressure brought to bear on these women, the lack of compassion and guidance shown them, and the failure to appreciate the lifelong consequences of forcing a woman to surrender her child. The similarity in the women's experience is movingly told by one:

> You know, it was such a long time ago and I started thinking, "Just let it go. Just let it go and move on," yet I couldn't, and I can't. It's a big issue to those who lived it. There are women out there who lost their firstborn child and never got to grieve. I can't even put it into words. It's a weird thing, this whole adoption thing where people think that someone could just hand their child over and it will be okay. Obviously, it's not. We're still alive. We're still here. We haven't died. Our issues are every day. We live this every day. (2006, p. 13)

With the poignant movie (2013) and book *Philomena*, by Martin Sixsmith (2010), and Marilyn Churley's more recent book, *Shameless: The Fight for Adoption Disclosure and the Search for My Son* (2015), the lifelong suffering of unmarried mothers and their relinquished children has been again highlighted. These women suffered the pain of losing a child and keeping the child's existence secret as well as the difficulty of ever finding out how their child fared in life. Gabrielle Glaser's book *American Baby* (2021) elucidates the effects of infant relinquishment on both mother and child. She tells the story of a teenage girl forced to give up her son and their subsequent determined search for each other. Diana Finley in *The Lost Twin* (2020) examines the impossible choice forced on a young unmarried mother to give up one of her twin boys, and its lifelong consequences for all three.

What also has become clear is the potentially deleterious effect of maternal abandonment on the development of a child's sense of self and of self-worth. For example, as Fessler notes, an adopted child can live in a fantasy world:

> A delightful girl … came to work for me when she was fifteen on a student program. She was adopted and she wanted very much to meet her mother. She … had made her mom a fairy princess goddess.

Another lives with negative feelings:

> An adopted girl had posted to one of the Internet lists and she was expressing such bitterness and anger about being given away and being discarded like trash.

Feelings of anger for abandonment are reinforced if searched-for birth mothers refuse to meet their child, react negatively when meeting the child, or are a disappointment, perhaps refusing to divulge important facts about background or health.

Yet not all effects are negative. A third adoptee develops a capacity for gratitude and compassion about what the birth mother must have suffered. "I have struggled with 'abandonment issues' due to my adoption."

She imagines,

> being anywhere with my biological mother, spending time talk-
> ing, getting to know who she is, and to thank her for giving me
> the gift of life. ... I understand in 1961 things were not easy for
> unwed mothers ... My [adoptive] parents love me and did the
> best they could, it hasn't been an easy life. I wouldn't change a
> thing; my life is full and everything I have been through has made
> me the strong independent woman I am today. (All three above
> quotes are from Fessler, 2006, pp. 291–292)

Fessler recounts a common fear of adoptive parents. Her adoptive
mother (Hazel) "feared I might prefer my 'real' mother to her ... " Sensitive to her adoptive mother's feelings, she waited for a respectable time
after Hazel's death to try to contact her birth mother. After much hesita-
tion on both sides, they connect. Fessler tells about the healing effects of
meeting her birth mother; knowing her parental and medical history,
similarities in their interests, that she resembled her father and that she
and her birth mother found common ground to talk easily, albeit with
emotional trepidation (2006, pp. 320–328).

The "shame" around pregnancy out of wedlock resulted primarily
from social and religious restrictive attitudes toward sexuality. However,
attitudes do not always presage behavior. Knott (2019) questions,

> What of the Dark Ages of sex implied by these recent stories of
> sexual revolution and of coming out? Was there really only an
> unrelenting, unchanging, silent world of coital sex before 1963?
> That seems like a caricature, or perhaps a myth, sex rarely being
> simply pleasure or simply procreation. ... the history of past sex-
> ual activities is almost uniquely hard to know. (p. 10)

What is known is that straightforward talk about sexuality, intercourse,
pregnancy has never been easy. Correct words for genitals, intercourse,
sexuality, gender, and so on appeared in dictionaries only with the advent
of the sexual revolution. It was considered virtuous, genteel, discreet not
to be able to describe sex. Even well-meaning parents, when asked, "Why

didn't you tell me more about sex?" would frequently respond, "I didn't have the words." Learning about sexuality is more common in schools (though not without traditionalists' resistance) through "Sex Ed" courses. Yet again, with each change of government, such courses can be further developed or threatened, depending on whether the government is progressive or overly conservative. "Sex Ed" may also be restricted in certain schools where conservative or religious parental protest is strong. Knowledge does not necessarily correspond with feelings, conflicted or otherwise. Despite increased knowledge, more freedom, correct words, changes in social and religious attitudes, difficulty in talking about sex can still result from the "shame" of discussing very private, intimate behavior and/or from conflicted unconscious meaning.

## Abortion laws and contraception

Abortion was not an option for the women who were forced to give up their children; it was illegal until the latter part of the twentieth century.[4] Until then, women for personal, familial, religious, ethical, societal, and legal reasons had to seek "secret" abortions, often at great expense and often risking their health, their fertility, and even their lives. With the Supreme Court Roe vs. Wade ruling, abortion became legalized in the US in 1973. However, with each change of government and Supreme Court composition, legal abortion remains under threat. Indeed, individual US states can still outlaw or limit abortion and at least ten of the fifty states currently do. In Canada, through a different governmental process, abortion was legalized somewhat earlier. In 1969, the Criminal Code was amended. Doctors, if a committee approved, were allowed to perform hospital abortions when the health or life of a pregnant woman was endangered. Otherwise, abortion remained illegal and a crime until 1988, when the supreme court of Canada found the law to be unconstitutional. In England, Scotland, and Wales, abortion has been lawful since the Abortion Act was passed in 1967. Abortion in the Republic of Ireland became governed by law only in 2018 by the Regulation of Termination of Pregnancy Health Act. Northern Ireland did

---

[4] There was no law against abortion (aborting a fetus through whatever method available) in the UK until 1880, in Canada until 1869, and the US until 1840.

not decriminalize abortion until October 2019. In each of these Western countries, legal abortion is not without some restrictions, checks, and balances,[5] and there remain some fierce opponents to abortion under any circumstances.

More recently, an abortion pill (Mifegymiso—a combination of two medications) has been developed. "It is highly effective in terminating a pregnancy and for patients less invasive than a surgical abortion; for the health care system, it is easier and cheaper to deliver. The regime of the two medications is on the World Health Organization's list of essential medicines" (*Globe and Mail*, Editorial, July 17, 2019). This essential pill is not yet readily available in a timely and guided way (Picard, 2019). However, with the changes in the abortion laws, more women are able to decide whether or not to give birth to a child.

Oral contraceptives became available in the early 1960s. In Britain, they were made easily available to unmarried as well as to married women but similar changes did not occur in the US until 1972. The section of the Criminal Code making it illegal to advertise or sell birth control methods was finally removed in Canada in 1969. (The then Prime Minister, Pierre Elliot Trudeau, famously stated that "the government has no place in the bedrooms of the nation.") Decriminalizing contraception gave all Canadians the right to choose to prevent pregnancy (and to protect themselves against sexually transmitted infections) without engaging in criminalized behavior.

The advent of the "pill" and other birth control devices (e.g., the "morning after pill"), the changes in the abortion laws, as well as the freedom of the medical profession to assist in family planning promoted a less judgmental attitude towards sexual freedom. A woman's right to choose pregnancy, the desired number of children, and single or married motherhood is greater than before. In fact, women are freer to choose to remain child-free without abandoning their sexual lives (see Heti's 2019 novel, *Motherhood*). Currently, the understanding of "normality" has also changed, most notably in the light of in vitro fertilization, surrogacy with or without parental eggs and/or sperm, and same-sex

---

[5] For example, abortion is permitted during the first twelve weeks of pregnancy, and later in cases where the pregnant woman's life or health is at risk, or in cases of a serious fetal abnormality.

parenting. A woman with resources can readily decide to have a child on her own (see Brockes's 2018 memoir, *An Excellent Choice*). Despite sexual freedom, legalized (though limited) access to abortion, and a more positive attitude toward pregnancy outside marriage, a women's "right to choose" is still not universally accepted or facilitated. Nevertheless, many women are parenting alone, particularly in Western countries, either by choice or circumstances. A single mother is any mother raising a child alone without the father's or partner's help whether she is unmarried, widowed, divorced, or separated. And numbers are rising.

## Prevalence of women mothering alone

Statistics show that in 2020, about 1.78 million single parent families (primarily mothers) were living in Canada, compared to 1.56 million in 2010; 30 percent of lone mothers compared to 11 percent of the general population live in poverty (https://www.statista.com/statistics/443342/single-parent-families-in-canada).

In the United Kingdom, there are about 2.86 million single parent families, with one in four children living with one parent. Nine out of ten single parent UK families are headed by a woman, according to 2020 statistics. Of all single-parent families in the United States, single mothers make up the majority. According to the U.S. Census Bureau, in 2020, out of about 12 million single parent families with children under the age of eighteen, more than 80 percent were headed by single mothers. Nearly a third of those families live in poverty and of the remaining two thirds, a great majority live in limited circumstances, with only a minority having sufficient resources.

Once mostly limited to poor women and minorities, single motherhood is becoming a new "norm" in the three countries at all levels of society. The increased prevalence is due in part to the decline in marriage, increase in divorce, and to the growing trend of children born outside marriage—a societal trend that was virtually unheard-of a few decades ago. Certainly, all mothering women, single or alone through other circumstances, need practical, social, and psychological resources if they are to care adequately for themselves and their children. Moreover, sole-support mothers, with or without resources, continue to be confronted with multiple difficulties.

Societal attitudes and social situations have changed since Hawthorn, Young, and Fessler published their books. Yet, today, many sole-support mothers remain in less advantageous circumstances. What do disadvantaged women, mothering alone, and their children need to live a productive, satisfying life despite inevitable difficulties? What does a woman need to achieve her own goals, to be less dependent on her child for her own fulfilment? The mothers in my study represent the numerous less privileged single mothers. They did not have the opportunity and sufficient resources to support themselves. What of their difficulties, their struggles, their strengths, their stories? What, from their backgrounds and current life situations, helps or hinders their capacity to be a good enough mother? This book will address these questions in the chapters which follow, but first, a description of my "research."

## CHAPTER 2

# The "research project"[6]

As already indicated, my interest in writing a book about mothering alone was sparked by the research project that I was invited to undertake by Project Chance. The board had been granted funds by the Chagnon Foundation for a project which would study the effectiveness and results of their program. The mothers in the Project Chance program, all with few resources, were provided with safe, secure, affordable housing while they were pursuing post-secondary education. Not only were individual apartments allotted,[7] with subsidized rent in a supportive community; for the children, basics were provided such as transportation to school, afterschool childcare, scholarships for children's private or special needs, as well as schooling and summer camp subsidies. Other services for the women such as book bursaries, a food bank, personal development and parenting groups, and an opportunity for

---

[6] A summary of the methodology, findings, and recommendations of the project are contained in Appendix II.

[7] The apartments were in two residences; the first and older one had twenty-one apartments and was established in 1989 and the second one, funded by the Chagnon Foundation, had twenty-three apartments and was founded in 2005.

discussion with professional women were made available. These services were added to the program gradually, were not readily available, ideal, or equally suited to all of the women in residence. However, the program in whatever form available at a particular time provided *opportunity* for all involved.

Since many of the study women themselves came from single parent, broken, and/or impoverished homes, and were without needed relational or societal support, an intergenerational cycle of deprivation and social pathology could be perpetuated unless there were *opportunity* to improve their own and their children's lives. For these women, as for all young people, education is a primary key to self-sufficiency and self-actualization. Few sole-support mothers can manage to balance the necessity of providing for themselves and their children while at the same time pursuing their education, let alone to the post-secondary level. Any women who manage to parent children on their own successfully, albeit with difficulty, usually have resources such as sufficient support, enough money, education, or a career which they are able to pursue while raising children. This does not preclude the (perhaps few) underprivileged women who somehow manage to find opportunity on their own and a way out of the intergenerational cycle. Many more suffer with their children through the hardships of poverty and deprivation.

The primary purpose of this research was to study the effect of the program; its strengths and weaknesses for women without sufficient resources. Those in charge and those funding the program wanted to know whether facilitating a woman's education and increasing her ability to meet her family's needs actually help. Which aspects of the program are helpful and what is lacking? A description of the study and its findings are contained in Appendix II. Quantitative (questionnaires) and qualitative (recorded and transcribed interviews) data were collected and analyzed for the purposes of the study. The study participation rate of over 93 percent of the women in residence and the sample of available alumni was sufficient to meet Project Chance's administrative objectives of the project. Only those in residence who participated in the first interview were offered a second interview and the participation rate (87 percent) remained high. What was learned about the program and about mothering alone is certainly not generalizable as a larger controlled study would be. However, my engagement in intensive interviews with these fifty-eight women provided valuable insights into the challenges of mothering alone. The interviews also allowed identification of the practical, psychological, and social factors that could support the ability to meet these challenges.

The fifty-eight study women were indeed mothering alone. Not all had been single mothers; some had been married and lost husbands through death or divorce; others had been in relationships which had not worked out due to abuse or incompatibility. All became pregnant in the usual way with a male partner. All decided to carry their pregnancy to full term and to raise their babies alone.

The quantitative data made it possible to identify four different vulnerability or risk groups: the low-risk ones, the restricted ones, those with moderate risk, and those at high risk. The characteristics of each group were as follows:

The Low-Risk Group had adequate internalized support,[8] strong coping skills, needing only a facilitating environment, assistance from others as requested, and encouragement to continue their relatively active and independent way of managing their lives.

The Restricted Group had for most a sense of self based on a strong identification with, or little differentiation from, their own mother. These women were low on independent action or lacked internalized support. To maintain their quality of life (including management of their increased emotional and physical symptoms), these women had to keep life stress to a minimum. They required privacy within a non-challenging, nurturing, and predictable environment.

The Moderate-Risk Group were neither at high risk nor had an independent way of coping, but were defined by various combinations of risk and protective factors. They were vulnerable to stressful life events. They required practical assistance and emotional support when their life stress increased and/or their social supports decreased.

---

[8] Internalized support is understood as the internalization of significant others brought into one's own mind as part of it (Akhtar, 2009, p. 150). It was related to secure attachment and high to moderate autonomy.

**The High-Risk Group** were insecure, lacked adequate social support, and were prone to acting on their feelings. They required special attention, extra emotional and practical support in handling life stresses, and sometimes medical and/or psychological care, especially when the achievement of their educational goal was threatened or their child experienced particular problems.

The low-risk and high-risk groups each comprised about one fifth of the sample; the restricted ones, the smallest, about one tenth of the sample and as might be expected, half of the women were in the moderate group. Their degree of vulnerability or risk varied with the amount of current life stress and available social support. Certainly, life stress was high for all the mothers but internal and external support varied considerably. Only the low-risk ones had internalized support. Alumni were proportionately distributed in three groups.

In summary, a woman's degree of vulnerability varied with her life stresses, internalized and/or social supports, identifications, coping skills, and attachment patterns. The "right kind of support" varied according to the nature of vulnerability. That is, the low-risk ones could request whatever kind of help they needed. The restricted ones, who tended to idealize their mothers, needed a private environment with little stress. The moderately vulnerable ones needed more support if their stress increased or supportive resources decreased. The highly vulnerable or high-risk ones needed constant support due to severe life difficulties and lack of internal and external resources.

The women's life stories were collected through the recorded and transcribed interviews which yielded accounts of their development in their own words. Although these stories could not provide the in-depth psychodynamic information that can be gained from patients in intensive psychotherapy, these women probably do accurately represent struggles faced by sole-support mothers with few resources in the community. Their experience also indicates how a program such as Project Chance helps by offering *opportunity*.

The women's stories unfolded each "in her own voice" in response to my opening question:

What gave you the courage and strength to pursue your education at the same time that you were responsible for raising your child?

The acknowledgment that each mother had inner strength facilitated a reflective, emotional, and forthright engagement in telling her story. As noted, most had come from financially and emotionally impoverished homes, had traumatic family histories, and were in difficult current situations; their pressing practical and emotional needs had to be met if they were to better themselves and support their children. Personal values, character traits, and circumstances led to the decision to be a sole support mother. Their children provided motivation to identify the basics required (income, living arrangements, childcare) and to enter higher education while mothering.

The hoped-for effect of the educational opportunity offered by the program was best summarized in one alumna's words:

It is not easy to be alone. Women alone with kids need support. If we do not have an education, we cannot give the best to our kids. It is the only way, otherwise, we stay on welfare and go lower and lower.

Personally, and professionally, I was interested in how the program not only met the mothers' practical needs but also promoted their cognitive, emotional, and social growth. Although the women in this situationally homogenous group were involved in a supportive program, I wondered if it were possible to identify challenges for women mothering alone as well as recognize some factors which contribute to their psychological growth and development. As a psychologist and psychoanalyst, I wanted to understand the women's innate resilience, the development of their autonomy and of their capacity to care, and especially their growth in self-esteem. This project provided the stimulus for me to speculate with my professionally trained mind about what can be learned, by women who are not in treatment, about women's development from the personal stories of women who mother alone and seek to better themselves through education. What can be learned from their backgrounds, the difficulties they face, their identifications, their recognition of their own and their children's needs that is applicable to today's mothering women?

Before the implications of an underprivileged mother's decision to mother alone and improve her own and her child's life through further education can be considered, it might well be asked: What does a mother have to provide to promote growth for herself and her child? That is, what are a mother's maternal tasks and what does she need in order to fulfill these tasks?

*CHAPTER 3*

# Maternal tasks

I t is common knowledge that those mothering must provide physical care, education, socialization, practical opportunity, and emotional nurturing, to promote the growth and development of their children.

> ...since humans are born underdeveloped, they can be educated and socialized to a far greater extent than any other animal. ... Humans emerge from the womb like molten glass from a furnace. They can be spun, stretched and shaped with a surprising degree of freedom. (Harari, 2011, p. 10)

As Anderson (2019) notes:

> Mothering isn't easy, and single mothering requires extra effort. In the end, we are all struggling to do the best we can. Perfection is a goal toward which we are working but which we must understand we will never attain. But we don't have to be perfect to be ideal. (p. 61)

Children can tolerate mistakes. A mother has to be "good enough," a phrase commonly attributed to D. W. Winnicott, a British psychoanalyst, and such mothering provides security, fosters self-esteem, and importantly expresses love for a child. Providing with love what is needed molds the child and promotes all-round well-being.

What are the basic physical and emotional needs of a child which a mother has the task of providing? Certainly, physical care, in general, comprises bodily and health care, adequate food, clothing, finances for the basics, a home, and eventually opportunity for socializing, education, and for growth of individual abilities. Bodily care includes feeding as needed, washing, facilitating and cleaning bodily waste, dealing with health issues. Nurturing care involves holding, touching, massaging, exercising, wrapping and freeing. Emotional care includes facial expressions, talking, identifying and sharing feelings, gentleness, strength, security, safety. Education and socialization begin informally very early "at mother's knee" and continue in appropriate formal and informal degrees throughout a child's life. Above and beyond the physical, nurturing, and educational maternal tasks, the ways in which a mother meets her child's needs contribute to a child's self-image and sense of self-worth. A "good enough" mother does not just provide a home but an environment in which the child feels secure and wanted; she listens for each child's expression of needs, at first reading nonverbal clues and gradually hearing words; she provides words for a child's thoughts, reactions, and feelings in mirroring intensities until the child can use his or her own words; she assures the child that she will be there to provide the child's needs. One woman's comments highlighted a mother's willingness, when necessary, to sacrifice for her child: "I had lost about thirty-seven pounds because I was eating peanut butter and toast and what was left on my daughter's plate but my daughter had good food."

A "good enough" mother provides physical care in a tender, gentle manner, showing with hands and eyes, pleasure and pride in the child's body; she identifies the gender of the child, accepting the child's gradual sexual development and perhaps differing gender identity; she provides a model while identifying and admiring the goodness, the individuality a child shows; she teaches respect for authority other than her own and encourages attachment to an available care-giving partner; she respects the child's wish to separate and be independent, which begins with the walking toddler's back and forth pattern—a pattern which continues throughout life and at first involves short then longer separations and returns until there is acceptance of self-care without parents who, finally, remain only in mind.

The mother, while remaining steady and caring, gradually teaches the child how to care for him- or herself. A mother relinquishes care in incremental steps only as the child is ready. A sensitive mother does so neither prematurely nor too late.

Many of the women participating in my study accepted their child's dependency on them as well as their striving for independence. They wanted to do their best for their children. Here are two examples: "I looked at my newborn and said, 'He didn't ask to be born, I brought him into this world, and I have to give him a fighting chance to be able to do something in his life.'" and "I was wild before I was pregnant but my family's values [internalized] and my religion supported me to become responsible and determined—I want the best for my kids."

Many of the study mothers recognized that each child is different. A "good enough" mother is attuned to these differences. Words of several of the mothers reveal their recognition that they and their children differ according to gender, age, and personality. Here are the words of women with one daughter: "My daughter is age seven, we have a good relationship but there is friction because she needs more time with me. I feel guilt, because I don't have a lot of time to spend with her." "My daughter is age eleven, approaching adolescence. I try to be protective and provide a secure relationship because I am worried that she will experience abuse in her teen years as I did."

Women with more than one child are especially aware of their children's different needs:

> I have a daughter age nine and a son age six. My daughter has a flamboyant personality; she talks, questions, and at times is smart mouthed but mostly a well-behaved young lady; my son is a "little devil," an active boy, doesn't sit still or listen but is friendly, likes to do his own thing and can amuse himself. He was operated on when three weeks old and hospitalized for three months due to a kidney problem but he is physically fine if he has no physical trauma.

Mothers alone with sons can find parenting particularly difficult. They recognize that their sons need a father and if a father is unavailable, their boys need male models. They try to make men available to their sons—brothers/uncles, their own fathers, accepting boyfriends. It is especially difficult to fulfill a son's need for a father: "My brother is here periodically for my son but they do not have a father–son relationship— it is a relationship more like a playful uncle."

Being a mother alone with a problematic son is even more challenging:

> My son is intelligent, easily bored, draining. With me, he was very aggressive, he hit, punched, bit, had a temper. His behavior increased after I separated from his father. When he was three, I called his father because I feared I would lose control of my rage. He continued to be aggressive and hyperactive but with his father was more receptive. My self-confidence as a mother decreased; my son and I needed help. He needs a father and that is difficult for me to provide.

Although it is commonly accepted that boys need at least a father substitute, the importance of a father to a girl's development is recently becoming better understood (see Benjamin, 1991; Harris, 2008). Many of the study women had some awareness that a paternal presence is needed for both boys and girls. Even if father is known, he may be there only intermittently. Both girls and boys can feel sad, even depressed, suicidal; both have feelings about father's absence.

> My daughter, age six, is competitive, does well at school, and likes to be with her dad. She lets out her frustration with me because she feels safe. Then when her father had a new woman in his life, she threatened suicide.

Mothers often are blamed or face negativity for father's absence: "My children blame me that their dad is not around. I am the bad one."

A mother wants her seven-year-old daughter to know her father and tries to arrange visits. Her daughter tries to manipulate at first: "If you don't buy it mummy, my daddy will," until her mother sensitively reminds her that her dad is rarely available and does not buy anything for her. And then her daughter struggles to accept his neglect: "He is not my father anymore because he changed his phone number."

At times, the father, though known, is unavailable to the child, which evokes additional reactions—frustration, mystery, fantasy, or intense clinging:

> My two-year-old son is mixed race. He sees pictures of his black dad but yearns for a father and calls others "daddy." He is very clingy with me, does not want to be in a room alone, he crawls into my bed, is aggressive with me, doesn't listen or do as I ask. He makes messes if alone but is not a problem at day care or with his grandfather. He craves a father and blames me for not having one.

A child's basic practical needs cannot be ignored by any mother but it is how these basic needs are met that promotes emotional growth—that is, is mom confident, is she clear, firm but flexible, is she stable and consistent, can she willingly and gradually relinquish care as the child learns to self-care, can she allow her child to find positive support and attachment in the outside world? Motherhood takes endless work, requiring energy, effort, thinking, organization, sleep deprivation, and self-sacrifice. A tall order for any woman, let alone for a woman on her own!

A mother is also a woman with needs of her own (e.g., a home, food, clothing, basics for personal care, emotional support, sexual needs). She cannot readily meet her family's needs if she is deprived herself. A mother can make sacrifices and all "good enough" mothers do. A mother cannot face unbearable hardship although a few do and survive with their children. In *Angela's Ashes* (1996), Frank McCourt tells the story of his exceedingly miserable childhood and of his desperate mother who had no money to feed her children. She had a husband but he rarely worked and when he did, he drank his wages. The children survived—they had a mother who, despite having no help, remained there for them. Yet the unhelpful husband and non-providing father stimulated the children's minds and imaginations with stories. Most of all, Frank and his brothers had a family and the love of their mother. After leaving home, the internalized, enduring mother was expressed in song:

A mother's love is a blessing;
No matter where you roam;
Keep her while you have her;
You'll miss her when she's gone. (McCourt, 1996, p. 357)

Although Frank McCourt came from an utterly impoverished family, his survival and success as a writer are relevant to mothers alone. His mother was persistent; she allowed access to his negligent father, whose stories stimulated Frank's capacity to write stories. More importantly, Frank's mother had intelligence, determination, and resilience, as do many of the women in my study, despite their troubled situations. These women, like Frank's mother, give their children what they are able to give—enduring love. Deprivation alone does not necessarily prevent development; many people have an innate capacity to develop within themselves, finding and accepting whatever degree of security, care giving, and stimulation is available.

For many women, however, education and work outside the home promote her interests, her self-expression. For sole-support mothers, such pursuits are not only self-expression but essential if a woman is to provide a decent standard of living for herself and her child. Yet no woman can easily balance her own and her child's needs alone. Nor should a woman use a child to meet her needs. Even mothers with providing husbands require daycare, housekeepers, or nannies to care for the home and children if they are to go to school or to work. Even stay-at-home moms cannot depend exclusively on their children to fulfill them. Few women can be adequate mothers without assistance or without interests separate from their children. What does a woman need when she chooses to mother alone a child she has brought into this world? What does a woman need to achieve her own goals, to teach a child to respect her needs, yet not be dependent on her child for her own fulfilment?

All mothers in my study were aware that they could not support their family through meaningful work or at a level above subsistence without further education and employable skills. Being a mother responsible for a child motivated the study women's decision to return to school:

I was at a dead-end job making minimum wage. I wasn't able to provide what my newborn would need with my dead-end job. That made me decide to go back to school.

My expenses were three hundred dollars more a month than I earned. When I realized I couldn't afford to attend university while supporting a child, a social worker told me about Project Chance. I was grateful.

Education has always been important to me but once I had my son, it was shoved to the sidelines. Then I married, things got rough, and the marriage dissolved. I knew that the best way to overcome my financial problems was to go back to school. Having a kid was good for me; I had someone to look after which gave me stability, purpose, and pushed me towards my goals.

I made the decision to go back to school, which my daughter's father did not support. It became unbearable living with him, we didn't get along and everything was my fault. We separated. I wanted something better for myself, a career, a chance to make money and help my daughter. I didn't want her to do what I did. I wanted her to go to school and have more opportunities.

What gave me the strength was my son. When I became pregnant, it was not about me anymore, it was about my baby. The birth of my son was the birth of me being serious. I woke up and took education seriously. I left a regular high school, finished two years at a special school, and graduated with an 84 percent average, moved on to college, took special care counseling, got my college diploma, and then while in the program began university.

Certainly, these mothers realized that they needed further education to find fulfilling work but the motivating push came from the desire to provide for their children. They had to find a way to balance mothering, home, education, and, eventually, chosen work. Mary Pratt, university educated, an artist, and at-home mother, described the dilemma clearly:

If one allows one's ambitions as a painter to soar beyond the reality of one's responsibilities as a mother, one must be frustrated with the resulting work. If, on the other hand, one surrenders to the housework and the household, there is an emptiness, a frustration which is no less real. What is needed is balance—an equilibrium. (Bishop-Gwyn, 2019, p. 83)

Balance is especially elusive for a mother alone.

Besides meeting her womanly needs, a mother alone has the additional task of helping her child gradually understand that she is a separate person with different needs. She does not have a partner who can assist her in meeting her needs and intervene with the children to "protect mom." As a child matures, awareness of mutual respect and responsibility grows. However, from the moment a child is born, a woman struggles between meeting the needs of her child as well as her own. Women in the study acknowledged that because they are alone, they had to teach their children early on that a mother also has needs. One mother cried when speaking about difficulties in both raising a child and pursuing her own goals. Another, whose daughter is "doing well" and is "responsible and caring," still had to explain to her child that she "also has needs."

As Knott (2019) notes, women "rarely wrote about the intense absorption of daily infant care" (p. 77). Nor were the women in the study asked specifically, "What was it like for you as a mother during your baby's infant years?" A few spoke without being asked about how difficult these early years were. Indeed, many stayed with the father or with family when due to difficulties in the relationships they would have preferred to be on their own. Being with someone even when the relationship was undesirable was better than being alone during pregnancy or with an infant; for a number, that was simply impossible. Here are two examples:

> I left home at twenty, saying to mom, "I've had enough, I have taken care of your problems but you treat me like a kid." When pregnant my mother pressured me to abort but I insisted on having my baby. We stayed with mom for six months and then I moved to my own apartment.

> During the pregnancy we lived with his parents, I worked full time and attended night classes. After the birth, my mother-in-law cared for the baby. There was mistreatment of my rare medical condition but I

decided to deal with the pain myself because I was determined to go to school. A year later, when my older boyfriend wanted to marry me, I was not ready to commit to the relationship and decided to separate.

As Notman and Nadelson (1993) note, "Wishes to conceive and carry a pregnancy and to deliver a baby do not necessarily reflect a grasp of the real tasks of parenting, with all of its accompanying changes and responsibilities." Yet, like most women not fully aware of the highs and lows of parenting, the study women decided to give birth. Ultimately, they decided to mother alone. Which motivations, which experiences prompted them to become a mother? What prompted these women? What of the quality of their relationships with their mothers, their fathers, their partners, and how did these relationships influence their decision? These questions require consideration and are addressed in the two following chapters.

## CHAPTER 4

# Becoming a mother

The wish to become pregnant is only rarely, if at all, stimulated by biological urges alone. It is commonly accepted that psychological and social factors accompany a woman's biological urges to become pregnant. Theorists now widely acknowledge that a combination of biopsychosocial factors contribute to a woman becoming pregnant and deciding to maintain a pregnancy until she gives birth.

Biological factors include hormonal changes, fertility, and age. Hormonal impulses and fertility are stronger when a woman is younger. The emotional influences leading to pregnancy are many and are only partially understood. A baby may be conceived and given birth for the simple reason of wanting to create a person—to create life. Certain other feelings such as loneliness, the need for companionship, hoped-for attention and care in later life, the wish to have a baby like oneself and/ or one's partner can contribute. The belief that a woman is incomplete without a child can be an additional factor. Socio/cultural factors such as gender role, familial and cultural expectations, continuing education, or work (professional or otherwise) also feature in the conscious and unconscious timing of the pregnancy. Thoughtlessness, carelessness, or naivety due to lack of sexual knowledge can influence conscious and unconscious motivations. Birth control may not be used or may fail. As well, forced or impulsive sexual intercourse can lead to pregnancy.

Moreover, it is commonly asserted that a woman's wish to have a child is motivated by the love of her partner. This may be true in many cases but not all. A marriage might be one of convenience or culturally enforced. A partner may be chosen to fill an emotional void. A woman may not want a child but her partner does and she feels it is her duty to give him one. She may not love her partner but still wish for a baby. The wish for a baby can be separated from a woman's relationship with her partner, just as sexuality can be separated from procreation. Motivations to become pregnant are usually both conscious and unconscious.

Is the wish for a baby "normal" within itself, with or without a loving relationship? What of a single woman? Are the contributors to the wish any different? Is it pathological because she is not partnered? Theresa Benedek (1951) insightfully commented:

> ... the term "unmarried mother" refers to a social status not to a psychiatric diagnosis ... (it is the) problem of the strength of (any [*married or unmarried*] woman's) personality whether (she) will be able to integrate all, (even) the regressive, gratifications of pregnancy into mature motherliness or whether she may be seduced by (them) [*psychodynamic factors*] into a psychosexual behavior which in our culture must be considered immature, harmful and even dangerous ... (quoted from Gedo, 1965, p. 352—italics the author's)

The wish for a baby as well as a woman's decision to mother her child seem to emanate from within the woman as much as from her life experiences and the nature of her relationships. A woman may unexpectedly become pregnant or knowingly try to become pregnant. Attempts to become pregnant can be numerous and take much time or succeed quickly with one try. A pregnancy may be planned or not, may be wanted or not, may have resulted from a loving relationship with her partner or a troubled, even an abusive one. If a woman is already in a relationship, the relationship may or may not be stable or over time might not work out. Reasons for a pregnancy can be as few or numerous, as similar or varied for a woman mothering alone as for a woman who is not alone.

What of the woman's experience of finding out that she is pregnant? Although the wish to become pregnant emanates from biopsychosocial, conscious, and/or unconscious reasons, in fact to date little has been written in the professional literature about a woman's reactions to learning she is pregnant or about her birthing experience. Knott (2019) documented that before the feminist movement in the 1970s, even physicians did not write, let alone speak, about a woman's pregnant condition in clear, straightforward language. Their notes included phrases such as "quickening" and "with child" to indicate pregnancy. Women, if noting pregnancy in writing, recorded similar phrases or more colloquial ones such as having a "bun in the oven." Now a woman can determine privately with tests whether or not she is pregnant. Still, doctors write little in their notes and women are only beginning to write about their reactions to pregnancy and their experience of giving birth. The pain of giving birth is frequently discussed but rarely do women admit that the experience can be exhilarating, in fact, an emotional high. However, for many, pain is quickly forgotten and the satisfying accomplishment is remembered. Balsam (2012) maintains that "the female body, and the act of childbirth that is the physical climax of its existence, have been breathtakingly marginalized and downplayed among clinical and psychoanalytic thinkers" (p. 4). She goes on to discuss the "tradition of female silence" about their bodily feelings and functions including pregnancy and childbirth, socially, medically, clinically, and even within the family, especially, astonishingly, between mother and daughter.

Feelings and bodily experiences of pregnancy and childbirth were not the focus of this study. The wealth of possible data and variety of experiences await further investigation. Fortunately, novels and memoirs written since the beginning of the feminist movement give some examples about a woman's wish to have a baby, her discovery of pregnancy outside a committed relationship, and her decision to mother alone. Two fictional women living in different eras come to mind—Clara in the 1930s from *Clara Callan* (R. B. Wright, 2001) and Dori in the 1960s in *The Tenth Month* (L. Z. Hobson, 1970) and another—a woman living in the 2000s, Camilla, from her memoir *this is happy* (C. Gibb, 2015).

Clara, a single school teacher in her thirties in small town Ontario, shocked the straitlaced community with her pregnancy and her "brave" decision to raise her baby. She became aware of her pregnancy while teaching:

> I felt myself on the verge of change. Yes, there in the ordinary moments of today ... I thought of transformation within the darkness of our bodies, when ... a human life begins. (Wright, 2001, p. 358)

A few weeks later:

> ... a harrowing sleepless night, but at four o'clock this morning I decided that I am going to keep the child. It was not yet day break but I could hear the robins. So, I am going through with this. (p. 364)

Clara describes her experience of giving birth:

> Yesterday afternoon, I felt the first pains. A friend phoned the doctor. ... the doctor was such a grumpy, old blister, but he helped me through the next nine hours, and I shall not forget his gruff kindness and sure hands. ... I was in tears when the doctor placed the dark-haired little girl upon my breast. ... And it is over and now I have a child and my life is changed forever. (pp. 405–406)

Dori was a reporter, a writer, and a ten-year divorcee who had not become pregnant because her body had not been able to embed a fetus. After ending one of her rare affairs without rancor, she discovers she is pregnant at age forty. Stepping out of the bath, she catches her image in the mirror:

> ... her breasts look fuller ... Below her navel, there was the faintest globe of fullness ... The moment she had imagined so many thousand times. Oh god, let it be true. (Hobson, 1970, p. 1)

Learning she is pregnant, she turns to her trusted physician and asks if he will help her through childbirth, though she is unmarried. He agrees and makes arrangements. During early contractions, she is supported by the few friends who know of her pregnancy. They accompany her to the hospital as the painful contractions increase. When the time to deliver arrives, Dori finds herself in an impersonal delivery room only with unfamiliar health workers, "to all of whom she is one more woman in parturition, faceless, nameless" except for a wrist strip with a number and false married name. Ten hours later, remembering little, due to heavy anesthesia, she learns from her friend that she has given birth to a healthy boy. Later, waking after post-birth surgery, unable to feed her baby due to necessarily bound breasts, she asks to see him. "She stared at the tiny breathing morsel … This sleeping being warm on her arm, this new life, this continuing of her life" (p. 232).

Camilla Gibb, a successful writer, at age forty-one, had an unbridled wish for a family. Stimulated by assisting in the care of a cousin's baby she realized that she could be a good parent with her female partner. "It would be the most important thing we would ever do in our lives" (2015, p. 74). After an unfortunate miscarriage, a healthy in vitro pregnancy followed. In the first trimester, disaster struck. Her partner "had lost her passion for me and that eroded her love for me" (p. 86). Unable to sleep or eat, depressed, at times suicidal, in denial, she tells no one she is pregnant. Though devastated, she eventually realized she had a life separate from her former partner. Her decision made, terror, denial, and aloneness are not over but integrated when she reaches out to a long-term friend to be with her for a necessary amniocentesis. Later, overdue and exhausted, she gives up natural childbirth and opts for an epidural.

> A second anaesthetist repeated the process a couple of hours later, when the first epidural refused to take. The midwife broke my water with something that looked like a knitting needle. Nothing was like it is in the movies [sic]. The contractions began to slow down because of the epidural. The midwife inserted an IV into my arm and began to administer oxytocin. To this point, I was disappointed in myself. I hadn't wanted this much intervention. A catheter was the final insult. (p. 119)

She loses her sense of time and place; she pushes with determination. "And then there was a baby ... in my arms. Bloody and bruise-lipped with black hair. Mine" (p. 120).

Paul Trad (1990), a psychoanalyst, drew attention to the developmental importance to a woman of becoming a parent:

> Parenthood, particularly motherhood, is one of the most common and powerful transformations in human experience. Recent clinical evidence suggests that the physiological and psychological transformations experienced by women while pregnant exert a significant impact on the relationship forged with the infant after birth. (p. 341)

One of the study women, as an example, confirms Trad's assertion:

> Many of my friends thought I might want to abort. If my mother had thought to not have me, I wouldn't be in this world. To decide that I don't want to have my baby was not right. I preferred to have her without knowing what she could bring to my life.

In my study, each woman's decision to bear and mother her baby was considered. As noted earlier, all of the women interviewed became pregnant through intercourse with a man. The nature of their relationships with partners was broached in the interview, as was their partner's impact on their decision to keep the pregnancy and mother alone. Their relationships varied from uncommitted, to unstable, to abusive, and to previously committed but now ended. What became clear is that once pregnant the woman's decision to be a mother by bearing and raising her baby was independent of the nature of her relationship with her partner. Furthermore, for each, the decision to mother her child appeared as a conscious choice whatever the underlying unconscious reasons or current circumstances. Even more deliberate and conscious were the women's decisions to mother alone in the face of familial, religious, or sociocultural positive or negative influences.

The women who had to decide whether to stay or leave an unstable, non-supportive, frequently abusive partner called on their capacity for independence and on their motivation to be good mothers. Here is what some of the women had to say about their decision to bear their children and become a mother:

> I had my child five years ago at twenty-one. His father and I had just started a relationship. We were to live together and I was to go back to school. I got pregnant; we didn't use birth control, because in my head, I wouldn't get pregnant—a self-destructiveness? I was open to having an abortion. I took several weeks to think about it and in my confusion, I found a name for my baby. I was taking vitamins. I saw the doctor, "in case I keep it." I realized by my behavior, that I wanted to have this baby. So, I decided to keep him. I was alone in making the decision; even though the father was there during the pregnancy. We separated when my son was a year and a half.

> I had my daughter when I was fifteen. That was hard, because I was young and my pregnancy was not well-seen in my family. It was an insult that a daughter would get pregnant. I was destroying my life. Both my parents were professionals and saw themselves as really straight people. Socially, it was not acceptable to them. I stayed with the father for six years. Then when I became depressed and he took out his job loss frustration on me with violence I had to leave him. Now, it is easier. My daughter is older; I am seen as serious, not judged as much by my family.

Those women who had been in relationships in which they were uncommitted, or in marriages which ended due to divorce, death, or emigration, faced different dilemmas as sole-support mothers. One woman, in an as yet uncommitted relationship, who unexpectedly became pregnant said:

> I wasn't supposed to be able to have children. I was twenty-seven and pregnant. There was no way I could have an abortion. This wasn't supposed to happen but I could handle this. Becoming a mom wasn't at all what I was thinking when I met this man. We had been together only a few months. I didn't love him. I knew I couldn't live with this man and left when my daughter was two.

A divorced woman explained:

> I decided to file for divorce from the father of my two children. My hair was falling out, bad things were happening. We were not having a relationship. It was just me with the kids. Why did I need to stay in a marriage if he was not physically or mentally there? I now have full custody with the legal parameters that we share decisions but he no longer participates in the children's lives. I decided to leave; I have to pay the consequences and do it all myself.

A widow left with two preschool children commented on her situation:

> The first year after my husband's death was very difficult and because of my mental illness I could not take advantage of the opportunity to continue my education. I had to leave the program and work in a low-paying job which did not require education to earn a living. Later, I had a boyfriend but ended the relationship because he didn't like the children. I had to work hard to raise my children alone and give them a good life.

Another separated woman told what happened after she emigrated:

> Although my husband had promised I could continue my education after emigration, he broke his promise and would not agree. I separated from him because I knew I would have to find a way to requalify professionally. By law, I was entitled to half of our assets but after three years of court fights, I decided not to continue and go it on my own. I wanted to concentrate on my daughter and my studies.

As these women spoke, I could hear their determination and satisfaction with their decision to keep and mother their children despite lack of partners' support and limited resources. Many of them led me to believe that it was the best decision they ever made in their life.

Beverly McLachlin (chief justice of Canada, 2000–2017) writes poignantly of a woman with whom she and others shared a house while in university.

The youngest of us was just nineteen and hugely pregnant. In an era when unwed mothers were often hidden and condemned, she bravely marched from class to class in bright tented dresses. She had broken up with her boyfriend in the spring, only to discover later that she was pregnant. We admired her courage and lived the drama of her choice. Would she put the child up for adoption, viewed as the "right" thing to do at the time? Or would she keep the baby? In the end, she decided to keep the child. A year later, I saw her with the baby, waiting for a bus. "Going great. Still studying," she said. And then with a frown. "Part time." I felt a pang for young mothers struggling to build a life. (McLachlin, 2019, p. 96)

Despite the inevitable difficulties of raising children alone, the three examples from literature had resources. Clara, dismissed from her work as a pregnant teacher, had her deceased parents' house, enough savings to last her a few years, and would seek less prestigious work but also less condemning than teaching when her child was old enough. Dori, due to her freelance work and an inheritance, was able to afford the cost of bearing, birthing, and eventually raising her child. Though the social attitude had changed and granted more quiet sexual freedom, little had changed in the attitude toward unmarried motherhood. Dori had to hide—resigning from her work—"to freelance," renting another apartment, and sharing her secret only with her brother, her best woman friend, and an understanding former lover. When her baby was born but she could not keep him, she had to wait until "the tenth month" when as a single woman she could legally "adopt" him. Camilla had financial resources as a writer and was able to buy a house—"We would live in this house and we would eat" (Gibb, 2015, p. 91). As well, she had the support of her mother during birthing—"I felt closer to her in this moment than I had ever felt or will likely feel again" (p. 119).

What was the outcome for these women with resources who chose to mother alone? Clara eventually finds work as a typist in a lawyer's office. It took three years and a labor shortage during the war before she got the job. Clara could not talk to her daughter about her real origins.

After the death of her mother and aunt, Clara's daughter discovers their letters which help her understand her origins, her mother's circumstances and decision. Dori's outcome is fairy-tale; the reader is led to believe that she marries her long-divorced obstetrician, providing a father for her son. Camilla, her child barely two, surrounded by a chosen family, successful as a writer, reflects:

> I have a job to do as a story teller; we all do. To tell stories that make us knowable to others, most importantly our children. To give them the tools to help them know themselves. And perhaps we come to know ourselves differently as a consequence. ... we become ourselves in relation to each other—visceral embodied—within us. (Gibb, 2015, p. 269)

Mothering alone is never easy, even with education, human support, and resources. What seems clear is that these women from literature, regardless of differing circumstances, decided to mother alone, having both resources and support. The young woman McLachlin knew in university seemingly had enough resources to make use of her opportunity. She was able to pursue her education, albeit part time while mothering her child. It also seems that the children of all four women are portrayed as healthy without special needs.

The young woman pregnant in university, empathetically recalled by McLachlin, provides a link between Clara, Dori, and Camilla and the women in my study. All three fictional women were educated in their chosen fields and had work. McLachlin's former roommate was able to pursue higher education part time and, like the women in my study with opportunity for further education, the long-term outcome is unknown.

Is it possible to mother totally alone without any resources, support, or opportunity? It is not!

> Human babies are helpless, dependent for many years on their elders for sustenance, protection and education. ... Lone mothers could hardly forage enough food for their offspring and themselves with needy children in tow. Raising children required constant help from other family members and neighbours. It takes a

tribe to raise a human. Evolution favoured those capable of form-
ing strong social ties. (Harari, 2011, p. 10)

Even with the basics, housing, food, this statement necessitating social
support, written about our ancestors (Homo sapiens) remains absolutely
true today.

It is well accepted that a loving maternal person and the quality
of a woman's relationship with her father affect the quality of future
relationships. What happens when these relationships are not ideal?
For a deeper understanding of the study of women's development, it is
important to look closely at their parental relationships as well as their
relationships with their partners, the fathers of their children.

## CHAPTER 5

# Parental and partner relationships

## Mothers

A woman's first model of mothering is her own mother. As Balsam (2000) notes, "Often it is only when a woman becomes a mother herself that she experiences the full impact of her own internalized mother" (p. 465). Chodorow (2000), quoting from her earlier 1978 influential work on the reproduction of mothering, maintained that "core psychological and interpersonal experiences for women can be understood in terms of internal mother–daughter lineage" (p. 339). The women in my study spoke readily about their mothers. Most had mothers with significant difficulties; often they were unavailable, or critical, even rejecting and abusive. These study women defined themselves as mothers by recognizing how they were similar to their mothers and how they were different, how they wanted to mother like them in a few areas but not like them in other areas. That is, as women grow, they develop their sense of self and their capacity to mother based on accepted and rejected aspects of the mothering they themselves received.

How did these women manage the quality and extent of their relationships with their own mothers to be able to mother alone? Did their positive maternal identifications have to be found with other mothering substitutes? What of the mothers who met material needs but not emotional needs? How did these women identify with some characteristics but not other aspects of their own mothers? That is, to what extent did they both identify and disidentify? The women's words provide beginning answers to these questions. Here is what some of the study women said about their maternal relationships:

## Quality and extent of relationships

My mother was not happy with the path I chose; she wanted me to finish my education and be married before having a child. She never got over the shock of me being unmarried and pregnant at twenty. We have a somewhat hostile relationship but she realizes I still love her. I am on my own now—no more hiding behind daddy or mommy. I have learned responsibility; I am the head of my household and have to be the strong one in my own way.

Although my parents were not married until I was thirteen, often they lived separately and I was moved back and forth between them. My mother still suffers from the downfall of her marriage and eventual divorce; she became more introverted and antisocial and retired early. Now she lives separately but upstairs from me. I resented her for a long time but now I am more of a caregiver to her since she's older and not going to change. I know there are more feelings inside me that I refuse to know now but as soon as I walked out of the doctor's office with a positive test result, I started planning for having the baby and going back to school. My aunt had provided the example of how to care for children so I knew what I had to do.

My mother's mother was overly involved with her but cared for me until I was five. I was traumatized when my grandmother left. With me, my divorced single mother was strict at first but became interested in men and then had little to do with me. I had to find my own way and now, though single, with two children, I have a family. Because my grandmother was so involved in my mother's life, my mother stayed out of my life. I let her know she needs to be involved in my life the lives of my children. My mother is changing and I'm proud of her.

These three women, despite having had poor quality or little mothering, found a way to be responsible for their children and even have some relationship with their mother.

## Mother substitutes

My parents left me with my grandmother who raised me until I was twelve years old. Growing up was hard because I couldn't understand why my mummy wasn't there. I wanted to find out why and asked but was told I talked too much. At thirteen, I was pregnant; my mother came back and insisted that I have an abortion. My grandmother said "No, you will have the baby; I'll be there." I had the baby and my grandmother stuck with me while I mothered; at eighty-two, she is still there.

My mother was not available when I was a child and is still unavailable. It was not my own mom who influenced the way I mother, but maybe it is her. I don't do what she did. My youth worker did many mothering acts, that is part of how I mother. Also studying helped me to learn what is good for kids and to understand my own mom and be more objective about her difficulties.

Mom wanted me to go in a certain way that wasn't what I wanted. She had an image of what I needed to develop my intellectual skills. What I thought didn't matter to her. My stepmother was easier to talk to; she didn't say do this or that; she listened and agreed. I am more open with my daughter; she is gaining autonomy and that is encouraging to me.

These women confirmed that women other than their own mothers could provide maternal identifications.

## Mothers and limited support

I had good practical support from mom. My mom was a determined person who raised us primarily on welfare. She worked and saved to send us to private school; she invested in her children. My mom was strict and I am. She didn't hug and I do. She had little time to listen to feelings but I listen to my son.

My parents worked hard and provided well materially but were emotionally abusive. My mom was strict, cold, authoritarian, at times violent, and I wondered if, frustrated with her marital relationship, she took it out on her children. I had to leave to get away from my parents' control.

Like these two women, others confirmed that their mothers could give practical support which were positive influences but rarely emotional support.

## Maternal identification and disidentification

I was depressed and read a book with a depressed character. I thought, I can't be like this anymore. I don't want to be like this woman in the book. I don't want to be like my mother. She uses her mental illness to victimize herself. I have a hard time speaking to my mother—tolerating her. I pity her. My personal growth ties in with my mothering; I want to grow—not to be better than my mother—but not to have my children think of me the way I think of her.

I grew up with a single mom, a university graduate, who left my father when I was four years old. She was manic-depressive and I have a dual image of her. She is an interesting, bright, charismatic woman, back working in her profession. She is also self-centered and won't help me. Though, like her, I am completing university. I know I have a vulnerability to her illness, but I am not my mom and I mother my daughter differently.

My mother influenced me most in mothering—in the sense that I try to impose on my son the strong beliefs, rules, regulations which she taught because they help in the real world. I am also different from my mom because I do not chastise him as she chastised me.

A pattern of identification and disidentification is evident. Many of the women disassociated themselves from the problems experienced by their own mothers. The degree to which they could identify with positive maternal qualities and to which they could differentiate themselves from their mothers' problems seemed to result in a stronger belief in their own mothering capacity. It was also evident that, for these underprivileged women seeking education, other women could provide a mothering model with which to identify, thereby filling some gaps left by their disidentifications with their birth mothers. Grandmothers, stepmothers, psychotherapists, social workers, disturbed mothers did contribute to the women's maternal sense of self. Sophie Freud (1991) confirms this possibility: "The intense yet painful bond with my own mother led me to search for better mothers all my life, and some of the deepest passions of my life were with other women, my second mother, my daughters, my first social work mentor, and my aunt" (p. xvi).

## Fathers and partners

Certainly, close relationships with men—paternal and partner experiences—also contribute to a woman's sense of herself as a woman and mother. A prime contributor to a woman's capacity for intimate relationships is her own father or substitute. These early paternal relationships influence the quality of a woman's relationship with her child's father who may or may not be her steady partner.

Traditionally, father was considered the representative of the outside world; mother was primarily involved in the home—the internal world. Although traditional roles have been maintained in some cultures, and families, it has become much more acceptable for father to be involved in the home world and in the basic care of children. Although this shift in the paternal role has been gradual, at the same time mothers have entered the workforce and are more involved in the outside world. This does not necessarily mean that all mothers work outside the home or that, for those who do, there is equal sharing of childcare by the father. Children need both a maternal and paternal presence to complete their sense of self and capacity for relationships. Increasingly, professional literature and research (e.g., Aisenstein, 2012, 2015;

Liebman & Abell, 2000) support the importance of the father as a con-tributor to a child's development, specifically, for a girl her maternal sense of self.

Freeman (2008) wrote, "Patriarchy is founded upon the symbolic power of the father and yet there has been a long-standing cultural silence shrouding paternal roles and relationships in experiential terms" (p. 113). Some of the current professional literature attempts to break this silence and address the role of the father in contributing to a daugh-ter's development and her capacity to mother. For example, as Spieler (1984) suggests,

> … the father is not a stranger and that the infant becomes aware of, interested in, and evolves mental representations of both par-ents concurrently and not sequentially. In the preoedipal period the girl needs reliable acceptance and nurturance from her father, not just from her mother. This enables her to form secure attach-ments to parents of both genders—attachments which serve as prototypes of the girl's relationships with both men and women throughout her life. (p. 63)

Boys also need male role models with whom to identify or disidentify (Diamond, 1998). All children need a reliable, consistent paternal pres-ence, a caring person who knows them as individuals, affirms, nurtures, and is emotionally involved.

Girls particularly need a father who admires and respects them as unique persons to round out their identification. A few of the women in the study had such a person, most did not. The question might be asked, does a woman's relationship with her own father (or father figure) pre-dict the nature of her relationship with the father of her child? Perhaps, but not always. Let's see what the women had to say about their own father and their child's father.

> My father was a hard worker and not much present. But he was more affectionate than mother. He hugged and played when he was there. My parents are still together, though they live separately, in a coun-try different than mine. I call my father weekly and have visited him several times. I married my first husband at nineteen; he wanted

children but I was not ready, and after five years we divorced. I met my children's father but when we moved to Canada he resisted my professional retraining. I left but he took me to court and, eventually, through mediation, I have full custody. Now I have a good practice and a good relationship with my fiancé and soon to be husband.

This woman identified with her father as a hard worker, placing primary importance on her education, her professional practice and caring for her children. Only then could she establish a "good relationship" with a man who is warm, supportive, and accepts her professional practice.

My father raised me to know that I need my own education because not all men are as committed to the family as he was. He was older when I was born. My parents are married for fifty years and are retired. I am still very close to my father. I am divorced from my husband but at the beginning he had visitation rights and he helped some. Then he stopped because he had a new family and we have no contact. When I left, we were living in a house and I was entitled to half of what we had but after three years of court cases, I decided to raise my children without his support.

This woman identifies with her father's view that education and self-reliance are essential. She could not remain with a man who was not reliable like her father.

My dad was more private than mom, quieter, calmer, a listener. I have his skill of relating to people in a more relaxed way. He was like rusty silver, quiet but good company. My parents taught me different skills but unfortunately my father died of a sudden heart attack when I was away and I never got to detach from him. My partner was, like my mother, up and doing, not ready to settle and be responsible. He could not be like my father. We separated when our daughter was six months old and he has no involvement with her; he is immature. I have a new boyfriend whom I want as a partner who can take responsibility. I am a responsible organizer but I have to sort out if I can trust him.

A father's way of relating is internalized and affects this woman's choice of a partner. She wants to be able to trust a partner as she trusted her father but fears loss and knows building trust will take time.

> My father worked out of town and was with us only four months of the year. Mom was the caretaker but I was closer to him. He was hurt when I became pregnant as I was his baby and I was having a baby. He wanted me to finish school but accepted my pregnancy before my mom did. As a grandfather he loves my son. My partner is "there and not there." I am trying to work it out with my son's father and he agreed to seeing our pastor for relationship counseling. I will see where that goes but I am planning my life without him.

Her father's acceptance of this woman's pregnancy and of her son helped her acknowledge that her father and partner had similar problems: "there and not there." She could then consider whether the relationship is worth working on. She also realizes that she has to develop independence, especially if she and her partner are unable to establish a steady relationship.

> My father left for another woman when I was in kindergarten. I saw him every other weekend; he partied and was drunk but never harmed me or my sister. My stepdad was racist, hit us and mom never helped. I had nobody, no discipline or guidance. I was with my partner at sixteen and became pregnant at twenty-two. He was in jail just after we started to live together; he had dealt drugs. It was an unhealthy relationship: he was controlling, verbally and emotionally abusive. Though he was interested in me, he didn't understand me. I realize it takes two and I am not a victim except when I was a child. We separated.

The traumatic paternal relationships this woman experienced as a child make it very difficult for her to choose a non-traumatizing partner. Yet she has strength in her awareness of her own responsibility.

> My father was absent and didn't take care of me. My grandfather was a great person, the only man in my life; he was a compensation for my absent dad. The father of my daughter is absent. I have a boyfriend

with whom my daughter has a relationship. He is helpful but emotionally we are very different. I am moving forward and he is not. I am not ready for living together and need time alone. I appreciate support and realize that I have difficulty with relationships but I am determined to plan my life. Independence is important to me.

It seems that father's absence and lack of care contributed to her "difficulty with partner relationships." Yet her relationship with her grandfather possibly contributes to her own determination and to her understanding that her daughter needs a father's presence.

My father was absent as he was a student in another city. My parents divorced when I was fourteen. I don't really know my father. I was spoiled by my grandfather who provided housing, a comfortable life. He was a military man, organized, calm, strong willed. We were very close as he helped me a lot; he took me to the mountains and showed me unusual things in the wild. He taught me to calculate, take risks, see opportunity and have the courage to take it. My problems with my partner began when we emigrated. I met him when I was working professionally; we married three weeks later and had our daughter shortly after. Problems accelerated here and we divorced two years later. At first, he saw our daughter once a week but did not help financially or otherwise. Now, he doesn't see her and I have no time for a man because my child needs attention and I want to finish studying before I find her a father.

This couple's problems began to accelerate after leaving their country of origin. She left behind the one man who was a constant in her life and with whom she was close—her grandfather. Her partner, like her father, was absent in their daughter's life. Yet, like her grandfather, she is organized, strong willed, and determined.

I grew up bi-racial as my mother was black and my father was white European. My stepfather was a white racist and Canadian. Though my stepfather was alcoholic, he was there to care for us and as far as I knew, he was my dad. My birth father was in my life until I was six but as my "godfather." My mother didn't tell me he was my real father until I was a teenager and I was angry with her. I have had several partners but none lasted. I have no partner or confidant now and do not wish for one.

Perhaps her mother's secrecy contributed to this woman's confusion about paternal care and anger about paternal origin. This, in turn, could contribute to her difficulty in trusting men and establishing a lasting partnership.

My father was abusive physically and possibly sexually to at least my older sister. I have vague feelings of abuse but no clear memory. A male teacher represented a man who was just human with insecurities but a good person. I trusted him enough to write a story of my past. When the course finished, I experienced loss of him. I had become pregnant at fifteen and again with a different partner, ten years later. Both partners left when I became pregnant. I realized that to be a mother alone is both generational and common where we live. In between my two children, I had an abortion because even mothering one child was too much for me at the time. I was not ready for a relationship then, nor was one offered. I am not ready now but I like men and realize because of my children, there can be no hitting or abuse in a new relationship. My children come first and a new partner has to be a hundred percent with my kids.

A father's abuse and the repetition of generational history contributed to this woman's early pregnancy and inability to choose trustworthy men. However, her good relationship with a male teacher allowed her to "like men" and grow in her realization that she and her children needed a trustworthy man.

My father was a "nut case," a criminal; he beat my mother. Before I was born, he tied my mother to a bed and broke her arms. He was so dangerous that my mother went to a battered women's shelter and later moved out of the city. My stepfather was shiftless and I never saw my birth father again. At first my partner and I had a very satisfying relationship. Only later, I learned that my daughter's father was a criminal. He was in and out of jail and had little involvement with our daughter. He was demanding, like a "big baby," and provided no support, financial or otherwise. I couldn't satisfy his demands and secretly managed to leave with my mother's help. He has moved out of the country and has no contact.

Was this woman seduced by a "psychopathic" man, initially charming? Was she repeating unconsciously her mother's history of having to leave quickly and secretly because of his verbal abuse and untrustworthiness? Possibly.

One story of the deleterious effect of parental and partner relationships was especially moving. How this woman spoke about herself and her son teaches us much about the importance of assessing strength despite a traumatic background and a son with serious problems. Her name will be Julia.

Julia, the eldest of three daughters, immigrated with her family when she was nine years old. Spanish speaking, she soon learned French and English. She was twenty-seven in her first interview and began by saying how privileged she was to have the opportunity to study and how determined she was to ensure a solid future for herself and her son. "I am an entrepreneur; I have a part-time business while I study." She planned her university studies and apprentice requirements to ensure employment: "In my field there is no unemployment." She commented on how proud she was of her son despite his difficulties.

> He is one of the best things that ever happened to me. I know it is better to have a child after finishing school and when you are a real woman. But, for me, it didn't happen like that. I was pregnant and married the father of my son at seventeen.

Julia sensitively described her son's difficulties. Her son, now age nine,

> has concentration problems even at school because though smart he has attention deficit. He doesn't do homework, disturbs other children, and lies at times. At home, he is immature, lazy, a bit overweight, has low self-esteem, and is confused about his father. I fear he will be held back a grade with no money available for a tutor. I am often at school late but he gets along well with his after-school

group leader. At times I am frustrated and impatient with him but reassure him that he is important to me. His father does not help and rarely sees his son now but I do not speak badly of him. I realize he needs a father, so I encourage his relationship as a friend with my boyfriend. It is a burden for me to study and mother at the same time because I have no mother or father to help.

Slowly, calmly, but with emotion in her voice, and eventually tears, she explained:

My father killed my mother. She was a wonderful person; no one deserves what she got. As a child, I defended her from dad's violence. My two younger sisters who were living with her called me at 2am the day she was killed. I was in shock but didn't fully realize it until I had to identify her at the morgue. The continuing pain of her murder makes me feel like it happened yesterday. Our relationship with her was as a good friend because she was young, sixteen, when she had me. She had three daughters by the time she was twenty.

We came to Canada for a better life. In our country, mom had been a stay-at-home mom but here she was home much less because she worked and at night finished high school. My father was a difficult man who didn't work and was violent with the children when he was home. He was evil, strange, hit us, yelled bad things, and I hated him, especially when he hit mom. He was also inconsistent and at times could be nice. He lived with me after mom left because he couldn't care for himself. With me he would yell and regress like a child; I set boundaries because he was not bad but sick. I had told mom not to speak to my father because he was violent with her but she was help-ing him with his income tax and gave him a lift in her car. He attacked her, she left the car but he followed and continued to attack her on the street where he killed her with a knife. He was sentenced to life with the possibility of parole in ten years. I thought about going to jail to pardon him, to try to put closure on what happened but I can-not because I am still angry.

My partner was violent and inconsistent like my father. I left him because I didn't want a life like my mother. He was also inconsistent with our son and often not there when he said he would be. I also cut off all contact with him to protect my son from inconsistency.

By Julia's second interview, a year later, both her own and her son's self-esteem had improved somewhat. She was focusing with determination on her studies and planning her own business using her skills (similar to her mother's). Although friendly with the other residents, she kept much to herself. Yet she demonstrated a capacity to relate and take in what she needed. She recalled what had helped her in our first meeting, that it was important to talk and cry about what had happened with her parents, her son's difficulties, and her relationship with men. She used the second interview to debate within herself whether or not to visit her dad. "I have nightmares; I don't like him, I am mad at him; if I pardon him, I am betraying my mother, I have very mixed feelings but he is my father." She impressed as an intelligent, strong, determined, entrepreneurial person who was capable of struggling with her mixed feelings. She used comments offered in interviews, demonstrating that she could relate to another person for her needs.

Julia's story of her relationships with her mother, father, partners, and son underlines the interconnectedness and profound effect of relationships with parents, partners, and children on becoming a mother alone. Because the interviews with women in my study were conducted within a year or two, it is not possible to follow the longer-term impact of relationships with a child. However, Sophie Freud (1991), herself a divorced mother on her own, wrote about the impact of giving birth to a child as well as the difficulties and pleasure which ensue over time.

> Nothing prepared me for the intense, fierce, tender, and passionate feelings that the birth of my first child unleashed in me. There was much suffering as well. Our love for each other became a chronic passion that caused us both difficulties for many years. Yet, while life is round, patterns need not repeat themselves in exactly the same way. My daughter is a more courageous woman than I have been. She started important conversations with me. Honest dialogue leads toward differentiation. Our love for each other has not become frozen. It continues to be difficult, but it is fierce and alive. (p. xvii)

A brief comment on the influence of the relationships between mothers and fathers. The majority of the women came from broken families and all had some difficulty in their relationships with the men who fathered their children. It is possible that the fact that their parents were not together could contribute to their difficulties with men in their lives. Coming from broken and troubled families could shatter an internal image of an intact parental relationship and likely contributed to their decision to mother alone.

As considered previously, sole-support mothers are confronted with multiple difficulties in fulfilling maternal tasks. All require basic resources and human support. Camilla Gibb, in a personal communication, underlines this reality. She wrote in an email,

> I am a single mother with good child support and good support in the form of a chosen family that has developed around my child, as I write about in my memoir. I am relatively privileged in these regards, where so many women whose stories need telling are not. (September 24, 2015)

Gibb, an educated (PhD), published author, able to provide for herself and her child, nevertheless struggled to overcome the difficulties of mothering alone but with a chosen family, professional help, including psychotherapy, she eventually realized she had the resources, the support and capacity to mother on her own.

The stories of the women in my study with few resources and little support or psychotherapy but with opportunity for further education require telling. The next chapter tells the fuller stories of examples of alumni and women in residence each from the different risk groups.

*CHAPTER 6*

# Life development stories

The following stories provide examples of the development of some of the women in Project Chance. The women's identities are protected by disguising names and personal details but with as little distortion of the important facts as possible. Seven stories within the four risk groups were chosen, at random, from those in residence and from alumni, as illustration.

## Women in residence

Four women in residence represent each of the four groups: the resilient or low risk, the restricted, the moderate risk, and the highly vulnerable.

### Low risk

Nancy typifies resilient women currently in residence. At twenty-one, Nancy "fell" pregnant when she had "just gotten the beat of going back to school." She and her older student boyfriend of four years at first decided on an abortion, because they had recently separated. The experience at the abortion clinic was unreceptive—"horrible." Although

57

the decision was painfully difficult, she realized, "I can't have an abortion and remind myself, 'my child would have been a year old now, or doing this at two years.' I will provide." Throughout the pregnancy, she continued her studies, delivered her daughter in August and was at school in September. Nancy responded to postpartum complications by dealing with the difficulties herself as she was determined to go to school.

Nancy and her boyfriend agreed to keep the baby and work on their relationship. Her family rejected her, saying: "You're not able to raise a child and go to school," and she was "kicked out" of the house. During the pregnancy, they lived with his parents. She worked fulltime and attended night classes. After the birth, her "mother-in-law" cared for the baby while Nancy continued school. A year later, not ready to commit to the relationship, Nancy decided to separate. She and her boyfriend continued as friends and he remains a father to their daughter. Nancy, focusing on completing her degree and unable to afford an apartment, heard about Project Chance from friends and applied for the program. Fortunately, an apartment was ready. Nancy commented: "Project Chance is definitely where we need to be. It is a comfortable place for my child to grow. It gives me the opportunity to do what I want and to finish my first degree." With several years left in the program, she struggled to choose between a practical and a more desirable graduate course.

Nancy spoke thoughtfully about the effect of family dynamics on her relationship problems. She had grown up in a verbally abusive family who reinforced a negative self-image. Her mother, a single parent for eight years, found parenting difficult due to Nancy's congenital medical problems. Her grandmother provided compensating parenting. In hindsight, Nancy understood her mother's harsh reaction to her pregnancy: her mother feared she would become the stereotype of a young, single, uneducated mother. She had worked to send Nancy to private school. The pregnancy was a "dishonor to her." Her biological father was absent, her stepfather a gambler, and her mother preoccupied with work. Most traumatic was the abuse by a stepbrother when she was fourteen. Bereaved after the death of her grandmother who virtually raised her, and with no one to talk to, her stepbrother offered a sexual relationship, saying, "We are not blood relations." When she realized it was, nevertheless, "incest," she was too ashamed to tell anyone. When she finally did, she was not believed, even blamed. Now, as she demonstrates her ability to care for herself and for her child, her family considers her "the responsible one" which is "amazing, because I was the most ill-treated one in the family, and now everybody looks up to me."

Nancy's high standards make her critical of the other women who do not take responsibility for their communal tasks. Although she ran into difficulty with some of the residents due to her outspokenness, she found support from friends, and sought therapy and assistance from a few residents and the staff social worker. The parenting program was also useful to her. Her daughter, barely two years old, is developing well, and benefits from a secure home and the Drop-In Child Care program. Nancy likes living by herself and appreciates the no-men rule. If she needs a babysitter, her daughter's father stays. She understands her inability to commit to a relationship as her need for time to mature. "Maybe I'll want to be with my daughter's father later, but I like that we're separate and trying to be our own persons."

Despite Nancy's traumatic background, her strengths are mobilized. She is thoughtful about her family's and her own dynamics, realizing her need to mature. Her daughter's father is supportive and her family now respect her. She is able to confront and meet challenges. She is self-sufficient, at times to a fault, but contains her difficulty with appropriate dependency by harnessing her own inner resources, mobilizing outside help, and taking opportunity when presented.

## Restricted

Debbie, a resident in her early thirties, is a good example of the restricted woman. Debbie thought she wasn't able to have children but became pregnant at twenty-seven. "This wasn't supposed to happen but I could not have an abortion. I had done things in my life; I could handle this." Becoming a mom wasn't what she was thinking when she met the man with whom she had been together only five or six months. She stated, "I wouldn't have chosen him to be a father. I didn't love him." Problems surfaced with the birth of her child. Money was tight as this man earned very little. They moved from her "loved" apartment; her car broke down; she gave up much to stay with him. She babysat another child to make ends meet. He complained. She reacted with, "Leave me alone!

I have two children during the day and my child doesn't sleep at night." She didn't sleep well for a year; it wasn't getting better.

Debbie knew she could not live with this man for the rest of her life and left when her daughter was two. Support was virtually nonexistent. An only child, her separated mom wasn't available and her father lived at a distance. Because the custody issue was unresolved, support from her child's father remained inconsistent. Once her daughter was in daycare, Debbie decided to go back to high school during the day. In this way she had more time with her child and through education would eventually be able to provide a better life.

After high school, Debbie was in a very bad space but as noted before, she was able to make maternal sacrifices for her child: "I had lost about thirty-seven pounds because I was eating peanut butter and toast and whatever was left on my daughter's plate. My daughter had good food." When she realized she couldn't afford to attend university, a social worker told her about Project Chance. She was grateful because "I wouldn't be where I am without this apartment."

Debbie did well academically. Her daughter, in a good school and daycare, is happy and likes her mother being a student. Debbie focused on her daughter and her studies. Now in her final undergraduate year, she is trying to decide how to do a two-year MA degree with one year left at Project Chance. "I am used to living like this but if I work before I finish it will be difficult to go back to school." She wonders if a master's degree will give her a better job. With high marks, she weighs her options carefully but with uncertainty.

Debbie's family history explains her need to reduce stress. Her father died at sixty-one of cirrhosis of the liver. In the last six years of his life, when he couldn't drink, he was excited to have a granddaughter and was a good grandfather. She was happy because, as a dad, he had been a loud, obnoxious alcoholic, sexist, racist, angry. Her parents had separated when she was four because her father was violent. She knew her father but grew up with a single mom who was a university student. Laughing, Debbie commented, "Patterns don't repeat themselves, do they?" Her mom had mental health issues (manic-depressive disorder) which, as Debbie explained, seriously affected her own development. "It was exciting to live with her when she was younger, because she was outgoing, energetic, a lot of fun, never boring." However, her mother's burnouts, suicide attempts, and the mental institutions "left me with post-traumatic stress syndrome and triggered my leaving home at sixteen."

Debbie learned to protect herself through premature independence. She found Project Chance when outside help became essential. Though distantly friendly with the women, Debbie depends on herself to maintain a focused, goal-oriented, "restricted" lifestyle, and keeps her internal struggles to herself. Because of her mother's mental illness, she realizes she is at risk psychologically. "Yes, I get sad or upbeat. But I keep it in check, due to my family history. I was not good at asking for help. When I felt vulnerable, like after my dad died, I realized I needed help so I sought therapy because I didn't want to get worse."

Debbie experienced insecurity within the family and developed early independence. She received little support from either family or the father of her child. She recognizes her own vulnerability, fearing she could be unstable like her mother and has some awareness of her identification with her intelligent, educated, sole-support mother. Due to her early relationship with her father, she avoids relationships with men, fearing they are undependable. She is focused, determined, intelligent, and ambitious but to reduce stress keeps tight control of her life and relationships; she asks for little assistance except when absolutely needed.

## Moderate risk

Susan, age thirty, always did well in school and would have progressed to higher education had she been well and had the opportunity and the resources. But, as she said, "I fell off the track and into a cycle of depression." Now, after living at Project Chance for three years with her seven-year-old daughter, she was about to complete her bachelor's degree in education and has enrolled in a master's degree.

Susan came from a large extended family of mostly single mothers on welfare. From age four she was cared for by her maternal grandmother because of her "mother's inappropriate lifestyle." Her grandmother, though very strict, provided a "good childhood": there was a routine and reasonable expectations. Her father was virtually absent but she had a positive relationship with her paternal grandfather. At sixteen, she went to live with her mother. Their personalities clashed; it was "a horrible experience." At eighteen, her mother moved abruptly, and "threw me out into the world." She managed to avoid welfare with unsatisfying work, which provided inadequate income and was below her intelligence. Alone and lost, she became involved in a dependent/love relationship. Once pregnant, the relationship deteriorated. He deserted her, triggering her depression. Desperate, she moved back with her grandmother, the "most important and supportive person in my life." She rallied. "I had this person growing inside me, I had a purpose." She gave birth and within a year she moved with her daughter to their own apartment. "It was the worst time financially," (she had no furniture, they ate at her dolly's table) but for her, emotionally, it was the best time. She said, "I breastfed for two years; we were attached at the hip." Then, the threat of welfare was a "siren call." She took a job with irregular evening hours, arranged childcare with relatives, and lived a "frantic" life. It was a time of stress, sadness, and guilt with little time for her daughter. Her work situation improved but as her daughter grew, she realized she also had to develop herself. "Every move I made affected this little person."

Evaluating her strengths in languages, she decided on a teaching career. When full-time university and paying the rent became impossible, Project Chance offered opportunity. Susan applied but "chickened out" because she feared the program would create an intrusive, uncomfortable dependency. After a year of part-time work and classes, the repetitive routine of getting up early, rushing to take the baby to and from daycare, cooking supper, going to bed, and feeling isolated, she decided to "sacrifice her independence and reapply because education was more important than feeling intruded upon."

At Project Chance, Susan's symptoms of distress decreased as success in university was facilitated. Her self-confidence increased. Her undergraduate degree was "not very stimulating," but now, in graduate courses, she realized her "training was not in vain. I acquired skills, I am proficient in my field, and feel great." Being bilingual, she is highly employable.

Susan has had a supportive man in her life for several years. Her separate space has allowed the alone time she craves. Her autonomy has been enhanced; she does not feel trapped or pressured into a relationship. She values the time to reflect on her relationship difficulties. "I'm a rough person, very blunt, which offends some people. I don't get attached easily, but I don't suffer from loneliness when I can relax and find creative ways to entertain myself." She valued the community involvement that she feared at first, and appreciates learning to live with different women. Her daughter has developed well and benefits from her interaction with the other children. When her daughter becomes sad and frustrated, they talk. To understand her daughter's reactions and feelings, Susan used her insight into the effects of their very close early years and her later withdrawal due to work. To ensure that her daughter is bilingual, Susan made use of a private school scholarship offered to Project Chance children.

Susan was in the moderate risk group. Although she functions well, she becomes depressed and less able to use her coping skills when support is unavailable. However, with the support of Project Chance, the stress of working and caring for a child is reduced and she is able to use her considerable intelligence to develop herself and work towards a better life for herself and her child.

## High risk

Maggie was sixteen when she became pregnant: "*a wake-up call.*" She realized:

> It's not about me anymore, it's about my baby. The birth of my son was the birth of me being serious about education.

When Maggie became pregnant, she was living with her mom, a single parent, and two sisters. Her parents divorced when she was five and her father was absent. Growing up in her family was difficult.

> I was taking care of my younger sister. My older sister did whatever she wanted. My working mother gave food, shelter, and clothing, but that's all. At home I was the good daughter (cooking, cleaning, caring for siblings) but I was skipping school, socializing, trying to fit in. My child put me back on the right track. I began to take school seriously.

Maggie's child is important to her: "my best friend, a good boy, not hyper, who listens well." She tries to give him what she believes a child should have, not because of what she missed but because of what he needs. Because of his intelligence, her persistence, and a child scholarship opportunity, he is now in an excellent academic school. She arranged through the court for her son to develop a supportive relationship with his father.

Education was important to her mother who expected her to focus on her studies. When Maggie became pregnant, her mother kicked her out. "It wasn't such a shock; I grew up understanding responsibility. I went to live with my child's father briefly." On her own for about seven years, she completed high school, college, and then commuted to university. At first, she took her son to school with her; there was daycare and she breastfed him in class until he was in school. They lived in low-income housing. It was lonely and very difficult.

Maggie happened on Project Chance; she noticed a sign with the phone number and luckily was accepted when the new building opened. Living at Project Chance, in a renovated building, was motivating and raised her self-esteem. She came home to a big clean, bright kitchen. It was energizing; they were no longer isolated. She had the chance to study, to focus, and to benefit from the help of the after-school program which her eight-year-old-son enjoyed. The staff was helpful but relation-ships with the other women were problematic.

> I feel like everyone else gets along together. I'm not one of the "liked" residents among the women. It's fine. I'm in my own bubble of stress which is a lot for me.

At the time of her interview, Maggie was in a transition crisis. She explained:

> I completed two and a half years of university. I became emotionally distressed making decisions because of my perfectionist problem and a need to accomplish. My mother wanted me to go to university; I wanted to show her and myself I could do it.

University was not for Maggie; she left for a community college degree in an art field she loved.

> I am distressed because I punish myself for not completing university. I just couldn't do it; my marks were declining. In the class, I thought only about art and decided to break my rules to do what I truly believe in.

Maggie is highly vulnerable without internalized support. Her severe perfectionism and self criticism, the stress of dropping out of university, failing to come first in an art competition and deciding to change course led to physical illness and depression.

> I was sad for myself, and disappointed for not finishing and for not making the right choices. My self-confidence decreased and my need for validation increased. With no one to support me, I handled this time of stress slowly, on my own.

She recognized that her talent had to be focused as "it feels so good to express myself artistically." She made the transition but "I'm still climbing out of my hole. I'm almost there. Hopefully, when I enter my new program, I'm going to be able to stand on my two feet."

Maggie exemplifies those women in residence who are highly vulnerable due to insecure attachments, low self-esteem, low capacity for relationships, and little sense of autonomy. She had to struggle with depression, overcome her perfectionistic tendencies, and identify her own educational goals separate from those of her mother. She also has a strong need for support which was seriously lacking in her life and was therefore at high risk. The opportunity provided by the program perhaps gave her enough support to help her "climb out of her hole."

## The alumni

As mentioned previously, none of the alumni were in the restricted group which is not surprising since the women who needed to live restricted lives most likely could not risk being available. Therefore, just three groups of alumni provide examples of how the women manage after Project Chance. That is, after they had an opportunity to further their education and received practical assistance while raising their children.

### Low risk

In her mid-twenties, Jane arrived from another country. She joined her husband who had promised to support her while she re-qualified professionally. She spoke some English but no French. Within three years, they had two children. When she was ready to re-qualify, however, she was expected to stay home. Nevertheless, learning two new languages, she returned to university. Her husband became more and more controlling, then psychologically and physically violent. She had to separate and called the police. For nine months, Jane and her children survived in shelters. It was very hard. Although her parents were not wealthy, they had provided what she needed. Now, for the first time, she had nothing of her own. She and her children were on welfare, living in one room; it was during the Montreal ice storm. Her mother visited for a few months, helped some, but Jane lost a year of university. Her children (nine months and two years old) needed her.

After repeated court appearances, the judge awarded her custody of the children because her husband had broken his written promise that she could re-qualify in her profession. While at the shelter, she heard about Project Chance and entered the program. Jane had found a facilitating environment and described her reaction:

> Oh, my god, I am going to manage, I am going to succeed. I have a low-rent apartment, each child has his own room, I have my room, and it is not far from the university. The director understands the women's situation, the supportive staff are non-intrusive. The daycare, the food bank, the social activities are helpful.

They stayed three years until Jane graduated.

What about Jane's background? She said,

> I had a happy childhood growing up in a village, not far from the capital. My parents, both engineers, spoiled us materially. I had education, a language teacher, vacations, summer camps. My sister, who is four years younger, and I were good children.

Her mother and father worked hard and the girls were alone until their parents came home, sometimes only at night. Their parents were strict, controlling, and gave materially but showed very little affection. Completing her education in her home country, she worked and lived on her own. However, parental intrusive involvement continued, providing practical help but their emotional support was never there. Jane speculated that perhaps she had to leave the country "to get away from my parents' control as I eventually had to leave my controlling husband."

What about Jane's life now? After graduating from a francophone university and qualifying professionally, she left Project Chance, opened her practice, and continued to support her children. She re-established a communicating relationship with her ex-husband, who now shares parenting decisions. Her girls continue to do well at school and Jane feels able to handle the stress of raising teenagers. Her relationship with her mother, who visits, has improved. When her mother tries to control or interferes with raising her children, Jane sets boundaries even at the risk of losing mother's helpful visits. She has a good long-distance relationship with her sister and father. Jane will marry her fiancé this year. Her life is on track, due to her hard work and ability to use the opportunity provided by Project Chance.

The qualities that define the low-risk graduates are readily demonstrated by Jane. She made the difficult decision to leave her husband, fight for custody, and constructively faced the hardships of being alone. She used what the program offered, and having felt occasional emotional care from strict father and mother's practical but controlling care, was able to internalize positive effects and understand the negative effects of her early life experiences. She is determined, resourceful in the face of life stress, and able to work productively and establish supportive relationships. She remains autonomous and modestly self-confident.

## Moderate risk

Mary was thirty-two at the time of her interview. She had three children, a girl aged eleven and twins—a boy and a girl—aged seven. At age twenty when she became pregnant, she had been with her partner for four years. Because they were "immature and stupid" she ended up pregnant and the pregnancy brought out the worst in him—"he was not bringing anything positive" into her life or that of her unborn child, only stress and problems. At that point she decided to be a single mom and left. She decided to seek a diploma in social services because it made her employable right away. It was not easy for her; she considered dropping out but continued for her daughter, asking herself, "Do I want to be a black, poor single mom and bring her into this situation? No." She was at Project Chance in the early days for one year when her first daughter was two years old. With the help of her mom and the year at Project Chance, she was able to complete her diploma.

After supporting herself and her child, she was accepted in an MSW program but deferred for three years because, "stupid me," she got married. Mary then gave birth to twins and after a few years went back for her degree.

Raised in a middle-class family—Mary's parents, both with careers, had emigrated from the West Indies and planned for a family of two—the first five years of her life were good. However, from five to eight her father became verbally and psychologically abusive to her "nurturing, loving, passive, self-sacrificing mother." These three years of her childhood were not good, with her father taking advantage of her mother's caring nature. When the abuse escalated to physical violence, her parents divorced. The divorce affected Mary "tremendously"—due to low income and loss of the house to father, they moved back to her mother's home country and family. It was a "cultural shock" and on visits, father used the children to manipulate the situation—he would buy what mother couldn't afford—and she and her brother made mom "feel bad" for a few years. Due to a political uprising, they were sent back to live with dad which was "torture." To protect herself and her brother from verbal and emotional abuse, Mary developed an assertive character and faced her father "head-on." She sought help from the school social worker. Advised to remove the children from their father, mother took her son back home and Mary, determined to finish high school, went to live with her aunt. Her aunt was not an easy person and Mary had little money to live on. She wondered, "Was there something wrong with me or am I surrounded by a bunch of wackos?" Despite this difficult situation, she maintained honor roll status every year. It was during this time that she became involved with her daughter's father from whom she eventually separated.

Later, after she married and her twins were born, Mary returned to university to continue her degree. Life stress accelerated: during her first semester, she started to lose her sight. Despite three children, an unsupportive husband, discrimination in her work situation, gradually becoming legally blind, she completed her two-year degree with distinction in three years. Other stresses included her husband nearly dying in a car accident and her daughter being diagnosed and treated for cancer, and difficulties with the children and her husband due to her decision to separate. Despite these stresses, Mary has a satisfying job and continues to work.

Mary's determination, characteristic constructive assertiveness, and high intelligence allowed her to succeed academically and engage the support required to deal with inordinate life stress. She commented that without her mother's help, the safe, subsidized housing of Project Chance, the support of other women in the same boat for the year of her diploma, she could not have persisted. She would not have been able to continue to work towards providing a satisfying life for her children. At the time we met, she was legally blind and highly valued at work. Though not ready for a commitment, she was able to attract good men and was exploring with other lawyers, some blind, whether her delayed plan of going to law school was feasible.

## High risk

Annie, her five-year-old son and two daughters, aged one and two, broke the isolation of poverty, loneliness, and single parenthood when they moved into Project Chance. The daily routine of caring for children and being a responsible student, however, soon became overwhelming. She reflected: "I and many of the other women had good intentions, but we didn't realize the juggling act of pursuing our education and being mothers." Within a year and a half, suffering from depression, in dysfunctional personal relationships, Annie left college and with her children moved into city housing. Was this "failure" or did she benefit from her Project Chance experience?

Sixteen years later, Annie at age forty-four, still single, now with five children aged eight to twenty, considers the influence of her life story and of Project Chance on their current lives. Desperate to stay off welfare and unable to complete a nursing course, she qualified as a patient attendant. Working at a low salary in a hospital, she managed to raise her children on her own. "The women in my family, though dysfunctional, don't carry their problems to work. When I work, I focus; I'm really good at what I do." Her "rich culture" taught her to "move forward, never give up and not to tend toward suicide" in the face of struggle.

Of biracial parentage and raised in a mixed ethnic community, Annie had a childhood of confusion and beatings. Her mother, described as a "mistress and an entertainer," married a man who was not the biological father of any of her children. Her mother's alcoholic and financially irresponsible husband was "a good father and as far as we knew, our dad." Confusion came from not knowing, until her teens, who her real father was. Confusion resulted as well from mixed feelings about her mother. "She was not bad, she provided food and clothes but she was strict; she beat and verbally abused us." The randomness of abuse led to low self-confidence, poor school grades, and later, abusive relationships and single motherhood.

At twenty, Annie left home. With little training, no financial backing, desperate for relationships, but with the wrong men, she had a "nervous breakdown." Eventually, pregnant with her first child, she resisted her mother's pressure to abort and insisted, "I'm going to have my baby." "I stayed home for six months and then I moved with my child to my own apartment." After bouts of depression and two more children, her "life was just a mess."

Annie's year at Project Chance gave her the support of the other women. Her children benefited from the safe environment and the exposure to different people, which contributed to their social development. Despite academic failure, Annie was determined to train and find work. She also increased her ability to find help. Annie has "no regrets" about having five children, or how she has conducted her life. She spoke in an empathetic way about her children's problems. Unlike her mother, she was encouraging, supportive, and non-abusive. She fought for her children's needs—her youngest daughter had learning disabilities—and Annie persisted until she found an appropriate school. As a responsible mother, she faced her children's difficulties. She was hopeful and there were signs that they would eventually sort themselves out.

Project Chance was a turning point in her life. She felt, however, that if she were to have succeeded academically, she would have needed prolonged individual counseling and tutoring. Such services were not available. She commented,

> Even if I didn't fulfill my academic goals, I achieved a lot as a woman by sharing experiences with other women who also had goals. Because my kids are growing up, I may soon be able to pursue the opportunity which should have been continued at Project Chance.

That experience showed me what I could achieve and where I could go in life. Perhaps I can be an example to other women.

Annie, a former resident in Project Chance's first group, illustrates the before and after life course of women in the high-risk group. Her background was severely traumatic. She was insecure in her relationships, lacked confidence in her abilities, had high life stress, and was highly dependent on outside support, not readily available. Yet there was a strength and determination in her. She pursued training for the kind of work which allowed her to support her children and care for all five of them. She valued her experience in the program and her improved self-esteem. Annie could not finish her education but she did not feel a failure and hoped for opportunity for further education when her children are launched.

* * *

These life development stories provide examples of the women's family histories, the nature of parental and subsequent relationships with partners, children, and others. The women's reaction to their histories and relationships, along with needed resources and the opportunity for education, contributed to maternal development whether or not a woman completed or left the program. Given their difficult circumstances and relationship histories the women in the study were all vulnerable but at different degrees of risk. Among the difficulties in their life histories which contributed to their vulnerabilities were: being raised by parents limited by their own problems, parental divorce, abuse, rejection, troubled personal relationships, deserting or abusive partners, as well as poverty and immigration. Many of their own mothers were overwhelmed by the responsibility of caring for children due to their own mental health problems, addictions, lack of support from husbands and often being single mothers themselves. Most of their fathers were abusive, absent, or unknown. As can be seen in what some said about mother, father, and partners, the quality and extent of their relationships also varied. A disturbing majority of their partners had no or minimal involvement with the child and almost all provided no or very minimal financial support. Certainly, life stress was high for all the mothers but internal and external support varied considerably. Family and other social supports were often inadequate. Their stories and comments exemplify their varying degrees of vulnerability from resilient to highly vulnerable, that is, from low risk to high risk. Yet, regardless of the differences in their vulnerability, they had strength to find a way to succeed. I wondered if they had certain characteristics in common which gave them strength.

Three characteristics came to mind: resilience, autonomy, and a capacity to care. Certainly, they were all caring for their children on their own, and were determined to find a way to pursue their education to better their own and their children's lives, thereby demonstrating resilience. They made efforts to assert their autonomy—their sense of self as a woman and a mother alone in her own right—by identifying and dis-identifying with their mothers. These characteristics and an attempt to understand their psychic development comprise the focus of Part II. This section consists of three chapters: Resilience; Autonomy, and Caring. I focused on these three characteristics because, separately and together, they are essential if a woman is to succeed as a mother alone. That is, they are essential to a woman's maternal growth.

# Part II

## Maternal growth

## CHAPTER 7

# Resilience

Much of the professional resilience research to date has involved children in an attempt to identify the resources and influences in their background and relationships that promote or inhibit resilience. Few resilience studies have focused on adults or have followed children throughout their life trajectories and their later functioning as adults. Moreover, to date, "The development of maternal resilience—the capacity for mothers to survive the vicissitudes of the parenting experience itself—has received even less attention" (Baraitser & Noack, 2007, p. 171). First, what has been learned about resilience to date? The resilience researchers best known (Garmezy, Luthar et al., Masten, Rutter, Ungar, Werner) worked primarily with children. Although Emmy Werner, especially known for her longitudinal studies, followed some of these children into young adulthood from birth to thirty-two years, she did not comment on maternal resilience (Werner, 1989).

Rutter considered resilience to be "an interactive concept that is concerned with the combination of serious risk experiences and a relatively positive psychological outcome despite those experiences" (Shean, 2015, p. 5). He maintained that competence must exist with risk for a person to be considered resilient. He recognized that individuals, even "competent" people, respond in various ways to adversity or risk and that "some individuals have a better outcome than others who have experienced a comparable level of adversity" (Rutter, 2006). The other primary researchers (Garmezy, 1993; Luthar et al., 2000; Masten, 2001; Ungar et al., 2007; Werner & Smith, 1982) all agree that to be considered resilient the person has to demonstrate a better outcome or adaptation than others in the face of similar risks, threats, adversity, or stress. Other researchers are also in agreement with this definition. For example, Clauss-Ehlers et al. (2006) note that resilience can be more broadly defined as a "process, capacity or outcome of successful adaptation despite challenges or threatening circumstances" (p. 125). In general, resilience research has shifted from an emphasis on mental illness to mental health and the factors which promote well-being.

There is also consensus that protective factors (internal and external) contribute to the growth and expression of resilience. Rutter identified four processes which protect people against the psychological risks of adversity: 1. Reduction of risk impact, 2. Reduction of negative chain reactions, 3. Establishment and maintenance of self-esteem and self-efficacy, and 4. Opening up of opportunities (Rutter, 1987, p. 316). He noted as well that the negative experience may have either a sensitizing effect or a strengthening, "steeling" effect in relation to the response to later stress or adversity (Rutter, 2012, p. 335). A primary protective contributor was identified as the caring support of relationships. Other protective factors include: "mental features, the parent–child relationship, social relationships (Rutter); high social economic status (SES), family cohesion and stability, and intelligence (Garmezy); maternal warmth, less separation from parents (Werner); secure attachment, normal cognitive development, effective schools (Masten); locus of control, expressiveness (Luthar); and (Ungar) self-efficacy, having a positive mentor and role models, culture/spiritual identification" (Shean, 2015, p. 27).

However, some of these protective factors do not always provide protection. For example, Luthar and Barkin (2012) found that socioeconomic status did not protect upper-middle class youth if they did not have a close, supportive relationship with parents, especially mother. Ungar (2008) was the only researcher to identify culture as an additional protective factor. He proposed that a culture was protective if members

shared values, beliefs, identity, and provided need-meeting opportunity. Luthar and Ciciolla's work on motherhood (2015) in their study of
well-educated women, the majority of whom had partners, found that
the women needed to feel unconditionally loved, comforted in distress,
authenticity in relationships, and satisfaction in friendships (p. 1812).
The work of Baraitser and Noack (2007) suggests that *maternal resilience*
includes the "aspect of ambivalence that entails bearing and accepting
ourselves as mothers (*warts and all*) as well as our ambivalent feelings
about our children" (p. 171, author's italics). Rich (1976) concurs that
a mother's ambivalence is inevitable: "My children cause me the most
exquisite suffering of which I have any experience. It is the suffering
of ambivalence: the murderous alternation between bitter resentment
and raw-edged nerves, and blissful gratification and tenderness" (p. 21).
I agree that awareness and acceptance of the inevitable ambivalence of
motherhood contributes to good mothering and a woman's comfort
with herself.

Winnicott (1960a), together with most psychoanalysts, maintained
that good mothering within a secure early childhood promotes healthy
development and protects against mental illness. There is no doubt that
most of the women in my study experienced poor parenting—either
maternal or paternal or both. Very few had a supportive parent—either
mother or father. All lived through serious risk experiences and had
to cope with multiple stressors. Recent adult adversities, such as housing difficulty, limited financial resources, personal relationship distress, and, for some, personal health problems and/or ill children were
widespread. Such adversity can result in increased difficulties in parenting. Furthermore, only a few had one or two of the strong protective factors (i.e., family cohesion and stability, maternal warmth, secure
attachment) outlined by the primary resilience researchers. These few
held onto the values and beliefs of a parent, a grandparent, a family rela-
tive, or had a strong cultural identity. Some had been given opportunity,
such as education, but practically none had the combined protective
factors identified. Most had to fend for themselves and find their own
opportunities.

However, there is much in this study which assists in understanding
resilience in a woman mothering alone. Determination, persistence, and
flexibility along with motivation and a sense of responsibility for a child

or children were characteristics which contributed to degrees of resilience in all of the women. Here is what they said:

> I was rejected from the program at age seventeen. I was not mature enough but I wasn't going to let it get me down; I continued school, took odd jobs, and a few years later was accepted.

> To leave my violent husband, I knew, I had to fight for custody, learn another language, redo a degree; I don't want to repeat my history of no love at home and broken relationships with my children.

> My parents abandoned me; it got very tough and I learned to fend for myself. I was determined not to have my spirit broken. As soon as I was pregnant, I started to take responsibility, to plan for the baby and going back to school.

> I separated from my unambitious husband and started school to retool.

> I was an obedient child, easy to love, a studious person with goals but raised myself. After I gave birth, I returned to school and later paid for my mother's return to school.

> I was somebody who was always doing something before I was pregnant. Then, after giving birth, my child and I were not getting anywhere. I had to make a move. I decided to separate and go back to school because sitting around is not my forte.

> I had to prepare myself for work other than low paid employment. I loved my job as a medical assistant but went back to finish high school and college to be eligible for university and eventually law.

> I always have to fight to get what I want. I know what I want and when I plan to do something, I am going to do it. I am very motivated,

> I wanted better quality employment with enough money to support myself and my daughter. I looked for an opportunity to finish my degree; I was ready to take responsibility.

My then partner encouraged me to go to university, but when I became pregnant, we separated. I continued school while pregnant, gave birth and returned to school though unwell physically. I was a parent.

I was pressured to abort but decided to begin my life with my child. I grew up with the idea I could have a career and be a mother so I recognized my abilities and decided to do a degree despite growing up poor.

Twelve of the women were rated as low risk but also had resilient qualities. Their resilience could have been due either to the persistence of prior resilient capacity or it developed during the program. Each of these outcomes is possible. Eisold (2005) noted that in the consulting room, she "came to know well people who have been capable of extraordinary resilience all of their lives" (p. 411). What other factors made these women resilient, given that they had few of the protective factors identified by the resilient researchers? It can be assumed that all of the study women had higher (or at least normal) cognitive development and intelligence, given that they were all enrolled in a post-secondary academic, professional, or trade program. Of note is that more of the highly resilient women were aiming for or had achieved post-graduate academic or professional degrees. High intelligence or distinct talent contribute to high achievement but do not necessarily predict resilience. Certainly, determination and persistent movement towards goals are strong coping skills. Along with determination are motivation[9] and a sense of responsibility. Independence in the sense of believing in and pursuing what seems right for oneself also contributes. Models and encouragement foster independence, especially awareness that it is right to identify and pursue one's goals. What of models and encouragement despite poor parental relationships? The women's words speak for themselves:

My mom and I were not close and she had serious problems but she went back to school when I was eight or nine and she always impressed on me the importance of education.

---

[9] Sandler and Sandler (1998) maintain that motivation emanates from internal and external relationships.

My mother left me with my grandmother when I was nine months for eight years but when she returned, we developed a relationship. Now she is very supportive. She had her first child at fifteen and had no time for education but pushed and encouraged me.

My father told me that I needed my own education as a woman to be able to be independent financially. Education would give me human dignity and psychological comfort. My independence has always been important to me.

My grandmother raised me and when she couldn't handle me, I had a "wonderful" social worker—I could talk to her; she knew me since I was eleven, she knows me and that I can do it; we still have a good relationship.

My parents left me with my grandmother and aunt. My aunt was my mentor, my rock; we were in a similar situation as she had to raise her kids alone, due to her husband's death. I followed her way of coping; unlike my mother, she taught me principles—honesty, hard work. She is still there.

My only family in my new country was a cousin and I didn't want to trouble her family. A very good woman came in my path—a Project Chance board member who treated us like family. Our director was also supportive. Strong women guided me with motherly advice to get where I am today. I was able to retool for my profession.

My daughter's best friend's mother is my best friend. The parenting group is also helpful; the leader encourages us to understand what our children need. Women striving for the same goal have similar expectations and the children know their mothers have to study.

It is quite clear that mothers, fathers, other family members as well as those outside the family, as models, can influence and encourage determination, and persistence, attributes which result in resilience.

The questionnaires and interviews of the study women were re-explored to compare them on the following factors: stress, loss, support, encouragement to do things their own way, self-confidence, depression, anxiety, physical well-being, children with physical or emotional problems, and cultural background. To identify and understand the factors which contribute to resilience, the twelve low risk women were studied in depth. Their rate of stress, encouragement to do things their way, self-confidence, rates of depression, anxiety, and illness in themselves and their children were very similar to at least two of the other groups. Only three factors (loss, support, and ethnic background) stood out for the low risk women and possibly contributed to their being rated as more resilient than the others at higher risk.

The twelve low-risk women had adequate internalized support,[10] strong coping skills, needed only a facilitating environment, assistance from others as requested, and encouragement to continue their relatively active and independent way of managing their lives. They reported little external support. The degree of reported support, even the number of confidants, is less relevant than the quality of the support, how it was acquired and how it is used. Those low risk women, despite stress, depression, anxiety, their own and their children's illness, and a higher number of losses to overcome, were able to manage the vicissitudes of mothering while studying due to their internalized support. They required less obvious support. That is, they had an internal image of being supported, even in the face of severe loss and other stressors. They believed support would be available and that they could ask for help when it was required. They were adept at identifying their needs and determined to meet them. What the resilient women needed was opportunity.

Those with restricted lives, even though successful and accomplished, were determined and persistent but less flexible. Many counted only on their mothers for support and consequently were less resilient. The resilience of a number of the other women fluctuated with the amount

---

[10] Internalized support in this study was related to secure attachment and high to moderate autonomy. Akhtar (2009) understood "internalized support" as internalization of significant others brought into one's own mind as part of it (p. 150).

of stress and available external support. That is, when their life stress increased and their support was felt to be inadequate, their coping skills or resilience decreased. Recall pregnant Susan, deserted by the child's father and depressed. Desperate, she moved back with her grandmother, "the most important and supportive person in my life." With this support, she rallied, "I had this person growing inside me, I had a purpose." She soon moved to be on her own with her child. Eventually, living alone with a child became too difficult. In time, she could accept the opportunity to improve her life offered by Project Chance. Without internalized support, mothering alone becomes too difficult. Adequate support in the face of increased stress improves a woman's capacity to mother while studying.

When stress was extremely high and support was literally unavailable, women in these circumstances had little resilience and could not manage the stress of mothering and studying. For example, one woman described the pressure she was under in caring for her children, studying, and working. The pressure became too much ("I became ill with schizophrenia") and she could not take the opportunity offered by Project Chance but had to drop out. It was only without the pressure of studying, effective medication, and a subsistence level job that she had enough resilience to care, with pride, for her children. Another had to change to a less academically demanding trade school to succeed in her own way.

The contribution of culture as found by Ungar was evident in one group—those women who came from the black community. It seemed possible that the greater prevalence and acceptance of sole-support mothers within the black culture contributed to resilience in a woman raising a child on her own. There is some evidence of family modeling, identity, and support as well as a certain "grit" or "street smarts" in what the women of color said:

> In my family, abortion was not an option. The attitude was "you should be responsible for your actions." Family means everything—we all do for our children. When I announced I was pregnant, the family were shocked at first then everybody was happy for me. None of us got married—mom and dad didn't marry but taught values.

I grew up the youngest in a large extended family and was bossed around a lot. Yet, I am the type of person who if I am struggling, I ask and assume that people will help. I was the first in my family to finish university. I wanted to be in a different income level than my family, have better quality employment and money to care for my child.

When I was eight or nine, I watched the news and learned that girls on the street were prostitutes. That made me afraid; I wasn't on the streets even though I became pregnant at thirteen. My grandmother gave me values—"You are not going to have an abortion. No matter what, I will be there." I try to give my daughter values learned from my experience, but know that she has to develop her own identity.

One time I ran away from my aunt who was raising me and ended up in social services. My aunt pulled me out, saying, "We take care of our own kids." I will always be respectful and grateful for what she did. She helped me become determined not to have my spirit broken.

My grandmother who was old and frail helped to raise me and sometimes my father, brother, and even neighbours but mostly I raised myself.

I understand now that my mother who had worked hard for me, kicked me out because she was ashamed when I became pregnant. She didn't want me to fall into the stereotype—black, young, single mother, uneducated. Now I am determined not to fall into that stereotype.

Responsibility for a child is valued more highly than marriage or a committed relationship within this culture. Those women who were not within the black culture also put their children first but mothering alone was less culturally supported. For them rejection of family ways to achieve independence was essential; "I had to leave to get away from my parents' control as I eventually had to leave my controlling husband." And "My birth mother hurt me, physically, and psychologically, but I learned from her what not to do." Another woman also rejected her mother's ways and said, "I don't want to be like her, so I do the opposite." Two women who were extremely close to their mothers became independent to protect their mothers; one didn't want to worry her mother who was in another country and did not tell her she was alone without support; the second protected her ill mother by never discussing her own difficulties.

All of the women aimed to improve their own and their children's lives. In the article on maternal resilience (Baraitser & Noack, 2007) the focus was on a small number of women in an open-ended therapy group lasting two years; the two women who left the group "were able to undergo the first proper ending process with the group, and, while they regretted leaving, the group fully supported their progress and was proud of their achievements." One of these mothers left to begin a course and the other to start working again. It is interesting that the "progress" of these two women in the therapy group had been achieved by all the women in my study—they were already pursuing or had pursued higher education. As noted previously, Masten identified the ability to think and solve problems as an important coping skill and aspect of resilience. All of the women in my study knew they needed help if they were to pursue education and they sought opportunity through Project Chance.

To summarize, although all of the women in my study were vulnerable due to their emotionally deprived, often abusive backgrounds, there were reasons why the majority were not rated highly resilient. The degree of resilience for forty-seven others in the moderate risk group was lower than that of the twelve women in the low-risk group and the degree of resilience depended on the availability of support. "Internal support" was identified only in the highly resilient group. Those in the small restricted, less flexible group had to maintain a much lower rate of stress, their children had fewer problems, and for many their primary support came from their dependence on a strong childlike attachment to their mother. The largest moderate risk group had a higher rate of stress along with much greater need for external support. They reported a greater number of people who gave external but often non-reciprocal support. As well, almost half of their children had emotional or physical problems which increased their stress. They also suffered more depression than many others. Yet when stress decreased and/or appropriate support increased, their resilience also increased. The high-risk group had higher rates of anxiety and were rarely encouraged to do things their own way—to be independent. As well, most of them found it difficult to complete their education due to high stress with virtually no adequate support.

Resilience, autonomy, and caring are in many ways intertwined, yet each deserves to be explored separately. The next chapter will explore the development of a woman's autonomy, followed by a chapter on caring.

## CHAPTER 8

# Autonomy

Autonomy and the self are intertwined concepts and lead to the phrase "autonomous self."[11] To understand "autonomous self," definitions of "autonomy" and "self" are needed. In common terms, "autonomy" is understood as independence from outside control with the capacity to act purposefully with intention, depending on one's individual thoughts (what is right for me), values, abilities, and situation. "Self" in the external sense defines a person as unique and distinguished from other people. Internally, "self" includes an image and feelings about oneself.

Before turning to what can be learned about the development of an autonomous self from the women in my research, I will comment on what I have learned about a woman's development of autonomy from my psychoanalytic clinical experience. The woman I offer here as a clinical example had achieved all external manifestations of autonomy.

---

[11] The phrase "autonomous self" is borrowed from the title of Jill Savege Scharff's 1994 book on the work of John D. Sutherland. Sutherland believed that "a distinct self is present from birth, and that an innate organizing principle guiding development of the self is present from the beginning" (p. 303).

She was educated, had married, had children, and had sufficient resources to manage on her own. However, as the analysis progressed, her external autonomy seemed "false," a cover for a lack of "true" internal autonomy.[12] It was through analysis of her relationships with her parents, her husband, and her inhibiting defenses that she was able to grow in her self-understanding and capacity for self-expression. She grew from a false to a true autonomy.

Gwen,[13] in her fifties, was a separated, professional woman with two young adult children. Her characteristic "pseudo" independence and disavowal of feelings became the central motif of her analysis. Like the "Little Red Hen," a story she had memorized as a child, when help was unavailable, she "did it herself." Gwen cared for others, ignoring her own needs. She was the second child and first daughter of a self-made professional father and an upper middle class, homemaker, but ill mother. Mother's eventual fatal illness and father's reactive addiction contributed to loss of parental nurturing. Brilliant academically, she gave up professional goals to care for mother. At twenty-two she married a man who achieved her own thwarted professional aspirations. She "chose" to ignore what she knew intuitively. Her husband's narcissistic hunger led her to adapt to his needs and to work full time while raising children almost single-handedly to maintain a stable family. Gwen's caretaking role superseded personal aspirations; being dutiful maintained her self-esteem, protecting her from helplessness and emotional isolation. She never spoke about her difficulties, even of her husband's leaving, to anyone, before she began analysis.

Gwen's analysis initially focused on her incapacitating depression over marital breakdown and low self-esteem. Through analysis, her

---

[12] True and false autonomy are similar but not synonymous with Winnicott's (1960b) "true and false self": "The true self develops in an adequately empathetic and caring maternal environment, but in its absence a false self evolves to protect the true self from adverse maternal influence. The true self is first present at the inception of primitive mental organization simply as 'the summation of sensory-motor aliveness'" (p. 149). It then becomes the psychological sense of the several ways in which a particular individual experiences himself as being "alive and real-authentic" (Bacal & Newman, 1990, pp. 191–192).

[13] Names, identifying information, and circumstances have been changed to protect confidentiality.

self-esteem somewhat restored and her depression no longer devastating, she actively divorced her deserting husband. The analytic focus shifted and a first dream revealed her central conflict: "My husband returned to our bed, he had his arm around me, I felt his weight on me increasing, I felt protected and held yet extremely frightened; I awoke in panic." She wished to be protectively held yet feared suffocation by duty. We connected her panic to the reality that despite efforts as dutiful daughter/wife, her mother had literally suffocated to death and her husband's emotional neglect and self-absorption had suffocated her ambitions and marriage.

As her analysis progressed, she began to understand her contribution to the marital breakdown (e.g., her passive-aggressive dutiful victim role). She commented, "My marriage had to be wrecked, I couldn't afford to keep up a false front and there was a solid self somewhere." Through recognition of feelings and analysis of her relationship with her transference mother/analyst, Gwen learned to accept not only her feelings of loss but also of anger and envy. As well, she eventually accepted her children's different lifestyles and choice of partners. She grew from a "false to true" autonomy; she commented, "I know I've changed; I feel this movement in me. OK life, here I am!"

Gwen's mother, though ill, provided the model of a meticulous housekeeper with which her daughter identified. Her father, university educated, was supportive but withdrawn. Like her mother, she married young, bore children, and became the dutiful wife/mother. Though successful professionally, with the intelligence and perseverance that could have permitted her to go further she could not allow herself to do so. Duty as daughter/wife/mother suffocated not only her personal goals but her feelings.

Through analysis, Gwen gained a "true" autonomy—a sense of who she is and how she got to be that way. She became aware of her identifications and disidentifications and of how her intimate relationship was affected by her upbringing. Eventually she could speak about her difficulties and feelings to close others and could allow them to help. She no longer had to "do it all herself." In time, Gwen valued herself more and recognized her needs as a woman separate from her children.

Unlike the Project Chance women, Gwen had resources and could afford the time and cost of an analysis. Despite her difficulty in talking about her internal self, and asking for help, her ability and determination "to find a way" led her to become involved in an analysis. The Project Chance women studied here had little opportunity for psychotherapy or psychoanalysis. Could they develop an autonomous self, to what degree, and how without resources and opportunity?

## Contributors to an autonomous self

Examination of the study interviews led to the identification of six factors which contribute to understanding the development of maternal autonomy and sense of self even without adequate resources. These contributors are motherhood, maternal attachment, adaptive defenses, resilience, the right support, and the capacity for reciprocal relationships (O'Neil, 2016, pp. 51–66). I discuss these contributors in detail below.

### Motherhood

Becoming a mother can be a contributor to the development of a woman's autonomous self. Trad (1990) underlined that motherhood contributes to a woman's autonomy and a mother's capacity to develop autonomy in her child: "After childbirth, the new mother undergoes further transformation as the infant begins to manifest developmental autonomy" (p. 431). In 1991, Trad comments further that: "The developmental transformations experienced by the woman during the antenatal and postnatal periods significantly influenced the evolution of an attachment relationship with the infant" (p. 403). I would add to Trad's statement that as a child develops toward adulthood and increased autonomy, a mother's sense of separation from her child and of her own autonomy changes as she contends with each phase of her child's and her own life.

Through motherhood, a woman becomes a mother in her own right. This is not to say that to develop autonomy a woman must have a child or become pregnant through heterosexual intercourse. Just as sexuality and gender have multidimensional structure, autonomy is complex, individualized, and relevant to women in all circumstances and all sexual orientations. Nowadays, it is acceptable for women to be child-free, and pregnancy is possible without heterosexual intercourse, that is, without a man but not without sperm. However, as noted previously, all of the women in my study became pregnant in the usual way and all decided to give birth to their children who would need mothering. Yet, giving birth does not lead automatically to mothering, to being a mother. Once a woman is physically a mother, she has to develop a caring capacity and, as the child grows, the ability to distinguish the age-appropriate needs of her child as well as her needs separate from those of her child.

Stuart (2007), in her study of "Work and Motherhood," had as her sample one class of university educated women with relatively secure social and economic status. Her sample included women in varying mothering situations: single, divorced, and remarried mothers; those who did not work for pay and those who were paid for work outside the home; those who home schooled; adoptive mothers; first-time mothers after age forty; mothers whose religious beliefs organized their mother-hood. Stuart made it clear that these advantaged women still struggled to find a satisfactory balance between motherhood (a child's needs) and work whether in the home or outside (their own needs). Even women, single or married, who had no children wondered whether they were putting their preferences (work or otherwise) selfishly ahead of mother-hood. Unlike Stuart's sample, the mothers in my study, without partners, with few resources, and mostly in low-paying work needed support for further education and better work.

Stuart asserted that, "A woman's ability to live comfortably within the realistic constraints of her arrangements around work and mother-hood is strongly influenced by the quality, extent, and management of her identification with her own mother. … What matters enormously is whether she [a woman] feels a deep, pleasurable sense of identification with her mother as a mother" (p. 454). Such positive maternal identifi-cation was rarely experienced by the women I studied. Some aspects of their mothers could be admired, other aspects had to be pushed away. In other words, they learned some ways of mothering from their moth-ers or mother substitutes and rejected others, in learning what not to do. They had to identify what for them was good-enough mothering. The degree of their maternal attachments and rejections influenced their sense of an autonomous self.

## Maternal attachment

Freud recognized the long-lasting effects of a girl's attachment to her mother and both Sutherland and Winnicott spoke of the traumatic effect of the deprivation of needed empathic responsiveness. Nancy Chodorow (2000) maintained that, "The internal world and sense of self are formed developmentally, mainly through unconscious communications between mother and child" (p. 338). To carry this thought further, Rosemary Balsam's paper (2000), "The Mother Within the Mother," describes the subjective experience of internalizations, focusing on the daughter's inner world as she confronts the challenges of herself becoming a mother. Most women become more fully aware of the impact of their own mother's way of mothering when they become mothers in their own right. At various stages of their child's development, they wonder, "How would my mother have handled this event?" or "Oh God, I sound just like my mother."

"Attachment to" and later "separation from" mother, are essential to the development of the autonomous self. Inevitably, there is an internalized attachment to mother, whether positive or negative. No woman can negate the impact of the woman who gave her birth. Even if a woman's mother dies in childbirth or early in a child's life, the child will wonder "What was she like and am I at all like her or very different?" An absent, neglectful, unempathic, or abusive mother often fosters a negative attachment, whereas an attentive, caring, empathic mother, a positive attachment. However, it is possible to develop an autonomous self with either a negative or positive attachment. Women with a negative attachment can assert, "I do not want to be a mother like her," and those positively attached can find qualities in their mother which they wish to emulate or not. A primarily positive or negative attachment does not deny mixed feelings about the best and the worst mothers. All internalized attachment to mother is always ambivalent but awareness of positive and negative aspects varies for each person.

Separation from or lack of separation also needs consideration. Complete physical separation from mother, though necessary at times, does not mean that mixed feelings are completely absent. Aware or not, feelings about mother are always with us. Even when a woman works at getting away from mother and her ways, awareness of similarities or identifications often come to mind in surprisingly unexpected ways. A woman has to work at finding her own way of mothering. On the other hand, a too close attachment, "I can't get along without her," or an idealization, "She was the most wonderful mother in the world," or "I want to be exactly like her," can inhibit or limit a woman's maternal self-development. Gwen's analysis, and the life stories and words of the study women also support the notion that true autonomy and sense of self as a mother develop through a process of identification and disidentification—balanced degrees of attachment and of separation. Autonomy and self-development are intertwined through degrees of security in similarities and differences. Knowing the impact of one's own mother, being aware of the nature of one's adult relationship with her and of her qualities as she becomes a grandmother, all contribute to a woman's emerging sense of herself as a mother and her ability to care for her womanly needs. Balancing children's and one's adult needs is always a struggle. As one woman in the study put it, "Like most women who are mothers, it is not easy to do things just for myself."

## Adaptive defenses

A third contributor is the presence of adaptive defenses. Vaillant (1992), among many others, stresses that psychological defenses can be either adaptive or maladaptive. Giving up maladaptive defenses for more adaptive ones is another contributor to autonomy. Initially, some defenses can seem adaptive but are actually maladaptive. To reiterate, Gwen's ultimately maladaptive defenses of pseudo-independence and reaction formation (caring for someone else as one wished to be cared for) were, initially, adaptive to her situation. Through reaction formation she put aside her own needs to care for her ill mother and then, her husband and children. Gwen had to come to terms with her dependency needs to develop more adaptive defenses; she gave up doing it all herself and became able to ask for help, to speak about her difficulties and feelings with close others. She felt freer, finding enjoyment in fulfilling her personal needs and taking pride in her adult children as they established their separate lives.

How does a woman on her own without resources achieve a balance between her needs and those of her child? How does she accomplish being both a student and a mother? That is, how does she care for her child and herself, practically and emotionally? What are adaptive defenses for a mother alone?

One of the obvious characteristics of most of the study women was independence. This was undoubtedly an adaptive defense. How else could a mother on her own, even without resources, provide for herself and her child if she did not at least value independence? To gain "real" independence through further education, each woman needed to and allowed herself to be dependent on the Project Chance program. Seeking out and entering the program required a degree of resilience and autonomy. One alumna realized that her autonomy was based on a combination of independence and dependency. Her parents' attitude had been, "I am giving you everything and I can interfere in your life and control you." For her, this expected dependency "chokes to death." Believing that it is "not easy to mother alone without education," she lived independently at a distance from her parents, put limits on her mother's visits and interference, and depended on the program for the opportunity to finish her education.

Other women in the study (e.g., Jenny and Vicky whose stories are told in the chapter on "Caring") also were able to give up maladaptive defenses. Jenny, as a young girl, had to mother her siblings, had to be altruistic, and prematurely feel she was capable of mothering. After a long struggle between her own needs and those of her daughter, she gave up her perfectionistic tendencies and realized she could find a balance among studying, having adult relationships, and giving her daughter somewhat more of the time, the affection she needed. Vicky, unable to parent her first child for several years, managed feelings due to severe trauma with self-destructive behavior. Only with increasing age was she able to cease self-destructiveness and become more comfortable with her assertive self. Then she was able to manage the needs of two children.

The next contributor—resilience—was discussed in the previous chapter. Resilience is intertwined with and important to the development of autonomy and of the self. At the expense of redundancy, more can be said about this inter-relationship. If a mother on her own cannot find ways of adapting to her situation, it will be very difficult for her to improve her life, especially with regard to education and work. She will also find it more challenging to develop her own autonomous way of mothering and of self-care.

## Resilience

Resilience is encapsulated, in Freudian terms, as the "instinct for recovery." In contemporary psychodynamic terms, it is the ability to assimilate traumatic or difficult events in one's life and their consequences which includes insights into the self and other. Gwen, following loss through divorce, committed to her analysis, learned to communicate more openly in close relationships, went on with her work, provided for her family, and eventually established ways to enjoy herself and her adult children. The women in the study found the program which supported their striving for further education to better their and their children's lives.

While Freud recognized the importance of the mother–child bond for subsequent maternal relations, he also believed that depression appears as fear of loss of a significant person and/or fear of loss of the person's love. Analysts today have developed much deeper understanding of the mother–child bond, its loss, and the effect on subsequent relationships. Many women who suffer loss also experience higher rates of depression. Gwen sought help because of her severe depression due to the loss of her husband. Although many of the women in the study suffered from emotional problems, primarily depression and anxiety, their symptoms lessened when they were supported and felt hopeful and less helpless. With hope, helplessness decreases and a woman feels less depressed. Opportunity through Project Chance offered hope to the women that education could lead to better lives for themselves and their children.

As one woman from the Middle East, compelled to marry an older man whose abuse forced her to leave for a "battered woman's shelter," put it:

> After years of feeling hopeless and helpless, unintelligent, unable to support myself and succeed in life, I needed to prove to myself that this was not so. I could not support myself and children on my current salary, I had to do something. No one in my family had a university degree. I decided, without telling anyone to apply to university and was accepted. I quit my job and my parents helped with the kids while I went to school. I became depressed living with my parents. Project Chance made it possible for me to be independent with my children and go to school.

Her courageous resilience is evident as she sought and found a way to succeed. Support, hope, help, and resilience are intertwined. In my view,

> *hope* is maintained or revived when it is realistic—possible to realize—when real opportunity is present and appropriate help is available from another person(s) or through self-help. *Hopelessness* ensues when one or more of the hope factors are absent and the person is rendered *helpless*. Hopelessness and helplessness are interdependent and opportunity is the intervening factor. (O'Neil, 2015, p. 214)

## Right kind of support

Support (internal or external) can come through life situations, life experience, opportunity, and/or psychotherapy. Support has to be sought and used to meet individual needs. Through identification of needs and the capacity to use available help a person receives the "right kind of support." As noted in my research, the women in the four risk groups from low, restricted, moderate, and high required varying degrees of support. Recall, the low-risk women had the ability to manage well, counting on internal support and the ability to seek and use help when needed; the restricted ones kept to themselves to reduce stress and most had unseparated or idealized relationships with their mothers; the moderate ones when under stress required much support from many others, even if at times, the help was superficial or unsolicited; and, those at high risk needed even more, often unavailable, help. Stanley Cobb (1976) in his seminal article on the buffering effect of social support wrote:

> Social support is defined as information leading the subject [woman] to believe that he [she] is cared for and loved, esteemed, and a member of a network of mutual obligations. There is considerable evidence that supportive interactions among people are protective against the health consequences of life stress. It appears that social support can protect people in crisis from a wide variety of pathological states: from low birth weight to death, from

arthritis through tuberculosis, to depression, alcoholism, and the social breakdown syndrome. (p. 300)

Cobb's belief that social support has a strong buffering effect was substantiated by the study women. They were especially aware of the support they and their children received from the program:

> I was able to go back to school and have decent living conditions.

> I am going to succeed. I have a low rent apartment not far from the university. I have my own room and each child has a room. The director understands the women's situation and the staff are non-intrusive.

> We are blessed to have this opportunity. The children don't feel strange because all the mothers are studying and we have the support of other women, those in charge of the program and those studying.

> I used to be so ashamed being a single mom. Then I noticed there were other girls like me. Some, like the stereotype of the single mom, stay on welfare and don't do anything with their life. Then, there were twenty-two girls with kids in this building, going to school and doing the best they could, surviving and making it. After a while, being a single mom became my pride.

A facilitating environment with similar mothers and approachable people is supportive. Additionally, the special programs for the children (e.g., school pick-up, the after-school program, scholarships, etc.) also assisted the mothers in achieving their educational goals. All of the women, depending on their individual abilities and particular needs, did not receive the same degree of support from the program, but even those who had to drop out felt they benefited. Recall:

> Even if I didn't achieve my academic goals, I achieved a lot as a woman by sharing experiences with women who had similar goals. My time in the program showed me what I could achieve. I do not feel a failure and I try to give my children opportunity.

## Capacity for reciprocal relationships

How does the linking of resiliency, autonomy, and reciprocal relationship add to the understanding of women's development? Often, independence and autonomy are conflated and dependency is excluded as a facet of autonomy. The challenge is to further develop psychodynamic thinking with regard to these concepts and to recognize that dependency is not necessarily incompatible with autonomy nor is independence equivalent to autonomy. Problems in relationships usually stem from problems in early attachments. However, autonomy is both intrapsychic and intersubjective. Autonomy includes both dependence and independence. One woman addressed both of these ideas:

> I understood that my husband needed control of his environment, of me, and I needed independence. Though difficult, we divorced. At Project Chance, the women on the board gave me what I never had in my life—a belief in me and encouragement—I learned to believe in myself.

"True" autonomy has to do with an inner sense of wholeness—a woman's capacity to grow in self-confidence/esteem as a person, whether or not she is in a relationship or desirable circumstances. True autonomy and self pride are not achieved without the capacity for reciprocal attachment. This capacity is not dependent on current opportunity for wished-for relationships. Opportunity for a close relationship is unpredictable. As well, in close relationships there is always vulnerability and the risk of loss. True autonomy and one's sense of self also include the ability to cope with the inevitable sadness due to unpredictable, even predictable loss.

Jessica Benjamin's (1995) ideas on autonomy provide support for the belief that true autonomy is not achieved without reciprocal attachment:

> The concept of mutual recognition includes autonomy—or, rather, preserves and transforms it as a pole of the necessary tension of independence/dependence between subjects, of differentiation. To oppose the idea of recognition to that of autonomy would deny the fact that recognition requires acceptance of the other's independence and unknowability. (p. 22)

## "Autonomous self" and mothers in my study

Having met with most of the women in my study on no more than two occasions, I do not have the deeper understanding of their psychodynamics that come to the fore in psychotherapeutic relationships. The capacity to constructively adapt to single motherhood, given their individual traumas, while at the same time working to better their situations and achieve some autonomy, was particularly difficult for these women. Although, as previously noted, most lacked resources, experienced poor, even traumatic, parenting, and had little opportunity for professional help, there is still some evidence that these six contributors were evident to varying degrees in these women's struggles to achieve autonomy. The alumni provide some information about the persistence of contributors to autonomous gains made at Project Chance.

The women in residence, mostly in the young adult throes of autonomous growth, demonstrate autonomous characteristics which they both brought with them as well as acquired through the program. Words from each of the groups (resilient to high-risk) provide evidence of how they developed varying degrees of autonomy. I was impressed by the evidence that autonomy was not dependent on which group a woman was in; the development of autonomy was evident in all four groups. For example, a resilient woman said, "At first, I was fulfilling my parents' dream, not mine." Now, she is pursuing her own dream. A moderate-risk woman who became blind during her first educational program is determined to pursue a professional degree, having been given support by others, who are also blind, in her chosen profession. A high-risk woman unable to complete her education commented that she focused on hard work, raised two children, and continues to support a child who is unable to be self-sufficient. She realized to achieve this degree of autonomy, despite her mental illness, she would need the help of "medication all my life." Another high-risk woman, due to her enmeshment with her mother achieved less autonomy: "I feel that I am too dependent on her. And if anything should happen, what am I going to do?" She could care for her son's needs but felt "helpless" without her mother and believed that no one else could help her. Other women, the "restricted" ones who were also very entangled with their mothers, tended to be less autonomous than the low or moderate risk ones.

I learned from the women in the study that personal strength, necessity, external (non-parental) support and its use, as well as the opportunity for self-development were additional contributors to the development of an autonomous self. Many of the women with these characteristics, completing their educational goals, also achieved a "truer" autonomy.

Motherhood as a life changing experience certainly contributes to a woman's "autonomous self." However, giving birth does not automatically make a woman an autonomous caring mother who can look after her child's and, eventually, her own needs. It is not easy for women who are mothers to do things just for themselves. Children take priority, especially when they are young. Moreover, autonomy begins in the family of origin and is influenced by parental identifications and disidentifications. Women develop their own kind of mothering as they become aware of the nature of the caring they received from their mothers, sometimes fathers, and in the absence of consistent parental care, from other caring relationships.

Sutherland, who believed in the presence from birth of a distinct self, maintained that the pleasure in their babies of both mothers and fathers assists in the development of autonomy (Scharff, 1994). Many of the women studied here were without the support of caring mothers or fathers or partners. Yet, as has been noted, many of these women as they became mothers developed degrees of resilience and autonomy. What about their capacity for caring? How, with less than "good enough" parenting, and often absent or abusive mothers, fathers, and partners, were they able to take pleasure in and care for their children as well as for themselves? Were they able to respect the gradually growing autonomy of their children? These questions are addressed in the next chapter on the development of the capacity for caring.

CHAPTER 9

# Caring

All of the women in this study made the decision to keep their babies and to mother alone. That decision involved taking the responsibility of providing each child with needed and age-appropriate care. They also made the decision to seek opportunity for further education in order to improve their own and their children's lives—that is, to be able to better provide. These decisions suggest that the women had a "capacity to care." They wanted to care, they decided to care, and they planned accordingly. The words "care," "caregiving," and "concern" are often used interchangeably. It is commonly acknowledged that concern is an important feature of social life and, by extension, family life. "Concern refers to the fact that the individual cares, or minds, and, as well, feels and accepts responsibility" (Winnicott, 1963, p. 73).

How did this capacity develop in the study women, given their lack of resources, their current life stresses, as well as their difficult backgrounds, including variations in their parental experiences and life situations as children? How was their caregiving capacity affected by the number, gender, nature, and problems of their children?[14] Furthermore, is the capacity to care inborn? Is it natural? Does the capacity to care need to be developed?

Anderson (2019) maintains that maternal caregiving is innately expected and normally offered. She writes,

> Our infantile selves seek security via maternal care. We seem to have a nascent anticipation that a care-bringing presence will tend to our earliest disturbance making it better. ... Further, close observation of earliest mother–infant interplay strongly suggests that mammalian evolution has hard-wired the expectation for a care-bringing presence. (p. 43)

Care for Anderson refers to the "object of this innate expectation, as well as the internalization of this capacity" (p. 43). To paraphrase, care involves the person who receives the care and the prior internalization of that capacity is in the one who gives the care. There is also some current evidence that oxytocin, considered the "instinct" of care, is at high levels after a woman gives birth and that this hormone is "important for the initial generation of maternal behavior." Additionally, "The brains of nursing mothers secrete both oxytocin and presumably endogenous opioids, a combination that can sustain satisfying, comforting effects for a long period of time. This may be why nursing remains such a pleasurable experience for many mothers" (Panksepp & Biven, 2012, p. 297). Oxytocin and opioids are also important in increasing caring and inhibition of irritability and aggression (p. 292). Although fathers often participate in caring for babies, "Mothers typically exhibit more natural warmth and desire to be with infants. It is also usually the mothers who more persistently carry on sensitive affective communication with babies, especially with happy babies but also with those in distress" (p. 299). This evidence

---

[14] There were forty-nine children among the forty mothers living in residence who participated in the study. Of these, thirty-one mothers had one child and nine had two children. The children ranged in age from five or under to nine with only six ranging from ten to fourteen. Boys and girls were approximately equal in number. All of them had been living in difficult circumstances. A quarter of the children (more boys than girls) were reported to have serious health problems.

that maternal caring has biological underpinnings does not suggest that life experience, learning through modeling, and personal attributes do not have a role to play. As with all human behavior, determinants include biological, psychological, and social components.

To illustrate this, the story of one woman, "Jenny," a woman rated as low risk and resilient, tells much about how she learned to care from several models, including neglectful ones. Her experiential and social influences likely sensitized her and, along with "innate" hormonal factors, contributed to the development of her capacity to care, which includes her struggle to meet the needs of her child as well as her own needs.

Jenny, age twenty-three, had a three-year-old daughter and was in her second year of university. She had been in the sole-support mothers' program for two years and was interviewed on three occasions. In her first interview, she spoke about herself in a matter of fact, emotionally integrated way. Living with and working to support her "irresponsible" boyfriend while also pursuing education, she became pregnant. With characteristic resilience she stopped school, had her baby whom she breast-fed, and within four months was alone with her baby, living on welfare. She had decided that supporting her boyfriend was no longer feasible with responsibility not only for herself but also her child. She didn't see her own or her child's life "going anywhere." Jenny sought and found the facilitating program of Project Chance and was able to return to her studies.

Throughout her second interview, Jenny wept because:

> I don't know to what extent I have grown as a woman. I spent the year pushing myself to meet academic demands but the better I do academically, the less well I do at home. An "A" means my daughter goes to grandparents or a babysitter. With me she watches TV, without the stability and cuddling she needs, so I can study. I tell myself I am right providing for the future, but I completely miss the present.

Jenny experienced sadness and intense conflict between motherhood and her own advancement.

Jenny described her personal history of abuse, neglect, and loss as "consistently—inconsistent." The home of her early childhood was violent and lacked basic necessities. Her parents, both substance abusers, separated when she was three. She did not see her father again until age seven. Within the year, she was placed in foster care and until eighteen she attended seven schools and moved thirteen times between mother and her foster parents. Due to mother's frequent absences, she parented her younger brothers—organizing, feeding, washing, and mentoring.

Jenny had a negative identification with her birth mother who deeply hurt her, physically, and psychologically. She asked, "Am I angry? No,[15] because I also learned what not to do and I learned a lot by taking care of my brothers. I am sad for my mother and for children like myself and my siblings." Although emotionally distant from father, she later developed some positive identification with him. Her foster mother—a nurturing, stay-at-home mom with constraining rules—taught the value of structure and loving support. Her foster father was also strict but accepting. Jenny used both positive and negative identifications to differentiate herself from the negative models of her birth parents and identify with the nurturing care received from foster parents. She said, "I found a balance as to how I would like to be as a parent."

By the third interview, Jenny empathetically discussed her own and her daughter's advancement. Despite a difficult year of her own physical illness, her daughter's severe asthma, the breakup of a love relationship, and marked conflict between mothering and her drive for achievement, Jenny lowered her exacting standards, and identified more realistic goals. As she drove herself less, she could give more time to her daughter. She had experienced the early absence of her difficult but not abusive father. Later, reunited with him—no longer a drug abuser—she learned constructive relationships with men are possible. Obviously intelligent (straight "A"s), persistent, and resourceful, with well-developed coping skills, she aims for a master's degree to teach underprivileged children (sublimation).[16] Growth in her caretaking capacity is evident.

---

[15] Jenny's "no" may have been "denial" as a defense but denial can be a relatively adaptive defense by "minimizing discomfort and looking for the good in difficult situations" (Vaillant, 1992, p. 272).

[16] "Sublimation," a mature defense, is defined as channeling or "gratification of an impulse whose goal is retained but whose aim or object is changed from a socially objectional one to a socially valuable one" (Vaillant, 1992, p. 242).

To understand Jenny's development, it is useful to consider her psychological makeup as it affected her progress toward caregiving. Jenny had the constellation of strengths that enabled her to be research-categorized as a resilient woman with a secure internal model of attachment, especially to her foster mother. Jenny experienced parental neglect and maternal rejection. She experienced anxiety and depression reactive to external circumstances (stress that was too severe for her adaptive defenses). She had both positive (foster mother) and negative (birth mother) maternal models as well as supportive substitute parents within a structured environment. She alone made the decision to raise her baby. To prove to herself that she was worthy and loveable, she used her intelligence to succeed at school, thereby developing resourcefulness and resilience early on and eventually her own way of mothering.

Balsam (2000) described the subjective experience of internalizations, focusing on the daughter's inner world as she confronts the challenges of herself becoming a mother. Jenny learned maternal caretaking by caring for her brothers, by disidentifying with her birth mother—"what not to do"—and by identifying with her foster parents. Unlike her birth mother, Jenny first took responsibility for her siblings and then for her child and thereby developed her capacity to care for others. She learned from her foster parents the value of structure and the positive effects of loving acceptance. She was able to identify and disidentify. Jenny's ability to deal with her ambivalence toward her birth parents and her foster parents, as well as her child, contributed to the growth in her sense of herself as a mother and a woman who could balance work (study) and caretaking. She grew in her ability to balance her own and her child's needs and worked hard, practically and emotionally, at doing so.

To consider further the development of the capacity to care, Vicky, rated as a vulnerable woman at high risk, provides a different, less straightforward, and more conflicted example. In contrast to Jenny who has one daughter, Vicky's children were boys, and she had a much more disturbed familial and personal history. Nor did she have the mediating presence of a positive foster family.

Vicky, age thirty, had two boys, ages four and fourteen, and had been in the program for one year when I first interviewed her. Her emotional vulnerability became evident in her response to my initial question.

She said: "I guess I had courage but for several years I was in a major depression from which I am still coming out." She had read the book by Wally Lamb, *She's Come Undone*, and after crying for a few days, realized, "I can't be like this anymore, I don't want to be like the woman in the book, I don't want to be like my mother, I have to do something to better my life."

Vicky's family history and her reactions lend some understanding to her being in the high-risk group. The middle child of three girls, in a family that moved frequently, she attended several new schools in a year, making her feel ostracized and without consistent opportunity to develop social skills. Father inconsistently changed rules and when she could "never get it right," she was predictably beaten. Her parents divorced when Vicky was twelve. Her mother, with the three girls, left a physically and possibly sexually abusive father, ostensibly to protect the children. Her older sister who ran away was under youth protection. Although university educated and in the helping professions, mother, obese due to compulsive eating, initially blind to the abuse, had a long history of mental illness, suicide attempts, and hospitalizations. Vicky was a lost child whose boundaries had been violated. She and her sister screamed out their pain by going on a "rampage of doing bad." Malnourished and discovering it was easy to steal food, Vicky's overweight problem began. At fifteen, she was pregnant, and had her baby at sixteen, refusing mother's pressure to abort. She said, "I was foolish to think I could handle it but I was determined to have the baby," albeit with difficulty.

Vicky's life became a mess—partying, drugs, alcohol, and acting out sexually, barely caring for her baby. Her older sister, now an unmarried teacher, cared for the boy for several years until Vicky could care for him. Then, deciding to get out of the welfare system, realizing her intelligence, she began university but again became pregnant—"an accident!" Although love/sexually hungry, she felt men were "horrible" as they deserted when they became aware of her pregnancy. Again, rejecting abortion, she decided to keep her second child as she was now ten years older and felt she was in a better place to be a mother. Vicky added, "I fell madly in love with my child." Her two boys now gave her a reason to better her life as she had to care for them as well as for herself. Although feeling guilt about neglecting her older son in his early years, she now made every effort to meet the needs of both her children, despite the difficulties and her personal frustration.

In Vicky's first interview, she blocked mother out, refusing to answer items on the questionnaire about her own identity in relation to her mother's. Sensing vulnerability from her evasive and distancing presentation, I focused first on the program. Initially, there was a bravado and defensive edge to how she spoke about the other younger women—their immaturity and foolishness. Rules were double edged for her. With some insight she recognized her pig-headedness and wondered if structure and accountability could balance her disorganization and uncertainty. Only later could we begin to discuss her troubled personal history and eventually she revealed a capacity for empathy.

I had commented that it seemed her mother had a needy, hungry childish part of herself. Vicky was able to use this comment. She related incidents of mother taking from her rather than giving but went on to explain that her mother had come from an abused background which contributed to her mother's problems. She showed understanding of how her mother got to be like she was.

Vicky was also able to assess her own current situation. Commenting on changing from a BA program to a college trade (furniture refinishing) program, she said, "I don't want to make things that are new; I want to redo what already exists." (It seems that, unconsciously, she wanted to redo herself.) With regard to men, she noted, "I am not ready for a relationship. I am concentrating on me, my kids, my school, and straightening out my own life."

By her second interview, two years later, Vicky was a thoughtful, calmer, trimmer woman able to reflect on a recent depression reactive to several losses and lack of opportunity: for example, the loss of structure due to finishing at Project Chance, having completed her course, the loss of support of a beloved teacher, and a wished for but as yet uncertain love interest in her life. Increased self-awareness without bravado was evident as was more realistic planning for herself and her children. After three difficult years in the program, Vicky spoke about her growth through emerging friendships with women. She had experienced love and loss of a man and now was gradually building a reciprocal relationship with another man. She was seeking therapy to address her childhood, realizing that she was "good enough" to use help. She now saw her life as a "sequence rather than a jumbled mess in my head." Although different from Jenny's way and from a more difficult internal and external position, she too was growing in her capacity to care for herself and her boys in her own way.

Anderson wrote that "Each of us learns to harbor a certain quality of this compassionate care according to how we ourselves were cared for" (p. 44). If this care is not available for whatever reason, the person may feel neglected. Yet, it is commonly accepted that each person reacts to various forms of care and to neglect in individual ways.

Jenny took responsibility early and perhaps realized what her brothers needed according to what she wished she had been given. She took on the maternal tasks that her unavailable mother did not. In the face of marked parental neglect and multiple moves limiting social continuity, she, apparently, had a strong innate ability to adapt. Her capacity to care was further developed by her stepparents' provision of structure and acceptance which allowed her to use her intelligence to pursue her goals. Attuned to her daughter's needs and a degree of self-awareness, she faced the conflict between high personal achievement and maternal caregiving.

Vicky, on the other hand, reacted to maternal neglect and paternal abuse by rebellion and self-harming behavior. Once pregnant, she chose not to abort—to keep her baby despite knowing she was in no position to give him what he needed. Her older sister, removed from the home and placed in protection against abuse, neglect, and self-harm, possibly had more care and greater opportunity to develop a capacity to care for others. Regardless, her sister had matured, was a teacher, and was able to care for Vicky's first son until Vicky was able to take him back. By the time she became "accidently" pregnant ten years later, she had matured to the point that she was able to abandon her premature, pseudo-independence to do her best to care for her two boys. Eventually, she allowed herself to depend. That is, she could receive help from Project Chance to further her education in a way that suited her, was able to establish social relationships with other women, and could seek therapy. She was also able to experience regret that she had not been able to give her first son what he needed. It is possible that her sister's care of her son provided a model of how a child's needs can be met. Like Jenny, she did not want to be like her mother, thereby disidentifying with her.

Recall that Julia, whose father killed her mother, kept very tight control on her life. She was rated as a "restricted" woman. Although she had suffered severe trauma, her mother had loved and cared for her compassionately. Julie idealized her and was highly identified with her mother. This care allowed her to try to protect her mother, feel compassion, and care for her severely disturbed father. Her internalized capacity to care (most likely learned from her caring mother) gave her empathy and love for her son within her restricted lifestyle. Both Jenny and Vicky spoke of hoping eventually to be in a loving relationship. Julie, focusing on her work and her troubled son, was cautiously in an intimate relationship which was positive for her because the man was a good listener, but also, he provided a male model for her son.

Susan, a woman of moderate vulnerability whose story was told previously, was cared for as a child by her "grandmother" who, in her eighties, continued to be there for her. When under a great deal of stress—alone with her infant daughter and few necessities of life, she fell into depression. Eventually, the awareness of her grandmother's continued presence and the opportunity offered by Project Chance lessened her depression. She was then able to use her intelligence to learn and to pursue a higher degree while caring for her daughter and son.

Even women rated at very high risk wanted desperately to care for their children. One woman, Joanne, described herself as poor. She wanted to break out of her family's cycle of poverty and single motherhood. She felt that single moms have to struggle to survive so that a child can live and can have what is needed. Survival was indeed a struggle. Having fought a drug problem, working to support herself and her child, sacrificing her education and her time with her child, she is helped to find Project Chance and return to school. Yet, her struggle continues; she barely has enough money, even with subsidized rent and student loans. Although a careful budgeter, after juggling to buy her daughter school supplies and good shoes, paying for tuition, rent, and her own books, there is nothing left over. She says, "Eventually, I will get myself shoes." Pleased to be in the program, have their own apartment, and be at university, her struggle increases as her daughter becomes severely ill, and both stop school temporarily. Despite significant anxiety she later persists with her education and caring for her daughter while knowing that even when she graduates, it will take much time to "dig out of debt."

How these women adapted to their difficult family histories is of prime importance in the development of their capacity to care. It seems that despite traumatic histories, and without the supportive relationship of a partner, their identity as mothers facilitated their caring capacities, their ability to seek opportunity, and their adaptation to challenging circumstances. Their current life stress—the responsibility of providing for a child—also stimulated their ability to use their capacity to care to the fullest. The opportunities offered at Project Chance went a long way in helping them with the most basic stressors by providing housing, finances to return to school, and, to some extent, food for themselves and their children. Even though their current situation allowed them to return to school, for most of the women, financial resources remained minimal and had to be tightly monitored. Very few of them had financial assistance, either from the father of their child or their own families. Many also experienced the stress of one or more losses over a two-year period. When their troubled backgrounds and personal relationships, especially with men, are taken into consideration the addition of a high rate of loss constitutes a significant level of stress for these mothers. Moreover, the emotional and physical health of their children requires consideration because the degree of severity of a child's problems also contributes to stress. If her children are not well a mother's conflict between work (study) and caring for an ill child becomes even more stressful.

## Children's problems

Anderson comments further that: "Bearing emotional storms, of course, can be wearing for even the most devoted mothering person" (2019, p. 44). A child's physical illness as well as a child's tenuous emotional state increases parental stress. Taking into consideration the variability in these mothers' vulnerability level, the problems of the children of Jenny, Vicky, Julia, and Susan illustrate the effects on the mothers' stress levels and their coping mechanisms.

When Jenny came to Project Chance, her daughter was three years old and by the third interview was almost six years old. During these years, much of Jenny's energy was also used to care for her daughter who suffered from severe asthma. Her daughter's illness necessitated hospitalization for some days every six to eight weeks. During these stays, her daughter was a "trooper," brave and a good sport. However, she expressed her frustration with her asthmatic condition by bedwetting and throwing fits. She was also slow in talking. Though it took her longer to speak, she eventually became articulate and talkative in both English and French. Jenny's daughter thrived at school and like her mother seemed to be extremely intelligent and sociable. Jenny, despite being torn between studying and mothering, and losing her patience when her daughter was rude and angry, worked hard to communicate with her. She encouraged her daughter's learning and physical and artistic talents.

Jenny wrote on her last questionnaire,

> My daughter's best achievement this past year was learning to speak French. From September to December, she didn't even want to go to school. It was difficult for her because she did not understand or speak the language. It didn't help that she was sick a lot and missed school. When she went back to school after the holidays, she learned to speak in full sentences. We are both very proud of this accomplishment and we often speak about how much she continues to improve in French.

Jenny's greatest difficulty was with her daughter's father who was very inconsistent in the minimal amount of time he cared for her. Her daughter's fits would often occur when disappointed by her father, leaving her feeling angry, bitter, mean, and whiny, trying her mother's patience. Jenny's family had high academic expectations for her which she also has for herself and her daughter. However, with the support Jenny now receives and which she is able to give to her daughter, both succeed with less internal pressure.

When Jenny was asked, "What gave you the capacity to mother when you didn't have a lot of consistent mothering yourself?" she responded,

> I've always been a mother, I was born one. At four years old, I had to bottle-feed my baby brother crying in the middle of the night. And I did. My mom would leave for days and I would be feeding my brothers. At my mother's place on weekends, I cared for my brothers when I was six, seven, eight, took them to the park, made sure they ate, had

their bath, were in bed on time. I did the same for my half-brother and sister at my father's.

It seems that Jenny was able to use her premature mothering capacity to understand her daughter's physical and social needs and help her to grow emotionally.

Vicky's two sons at the time of her first interview were fourteen years and four years old. Her first son was initially cared for by her sister, as Vicky, who had no support or resources, was not ready to mother at sixteen. Several years later, she had her son live with her, perhaps prematurely, because she still had more of her "wildness to get out." Eventually she worked and learned to mother—as she said, "to be both mom and dad." As a young adolescent, her eldest son became very difficult with no respect for his mother.

> He spoke to me in a way I could not tolerate and I had to make sure he didn't get out of control. He tried to be the man of the house and I would say, "No, you're not the man of the house, I am mother and father. You are a young boy." His behavior was completely disrespectful, rude, ignorant, hostile, and aggressive. One day he lunged at me. I punched him in the eye which gave him a giant bruise. It was awful and I am not proud of myself but it changed him, his behavior, his disrespect, and aggression towards me. He learned boundaries and to contain himself.

Guilty for deserting her first son, being wild in her early years, but growing in self-awareness and self-containment, and deciding on training that suited her, she feels more able to mother her boys alone as she is "not ready for a man in my life." Consequently, her boys do not have a father figure, their only male models being the workers at Project Chance. Her older son struggles academically but she encourages him to find training and work that suits him. Her younger son, now six years old, bright and good at school, appeared to be growing well. His occasional "dramatic tantrums" required "a lot of work" but she became more able to give him the attention he needs.

Vicky, with her own growing to do, was rated at high risk, due to lack of support, internal and external, parental neglect (paternal abuse, maternal mental illness), proneness to depression, acting out feelings, obesity, the stress of loss, and financial difficulty. She had her hands full parenting alone two active boys with markedly different age-appropriate needs. Her capacity to care grew as she grew.

Julia, the example of a "restricted" woman, had one son nine years old when she began at Project Chance. Initially, she had high hopes for her son: "My son knows that I'm studying and he knows my goals are his goals too. So, when I have good marks, it's his marks too because he's helping me to my goals—our goals." She recognized her son's difficulties with learning languages "not because he's not smart but because he's lazy." Her own high standards and her drive to better their lives were imposed on him in a near symbiotic relationship. Only later was she able to recognize that he had severe problems with concentration. Her own anxiety about not having him end up like her sisters—underachieving in special needs classes—and lack of money to give him the special tutoring he needed to progress in school left her feeling she was "a bad mother." She reacted to her son's emotional problems as she had to her father's severe problems—feeling that she was a "bad daughter/mother" and to blame for his disturbance. Being a "restricted" woman had to do with circumstances and self-protection: prior to our interviews she felt she had no one with whom she could talk openly; and her determination to make a life different from her family of origin necessitated keeping her own counsel. It bodes well for her and her son that she could use constructively my comments, had entrepreneurial ability (her own successful business while a student), was able to accept help offered for further education, and from a new relationship with a seemingly supportive man sensitive to her and her son's needs. Also, she could discuss alternatives for getting her son the help he needed as she realized gradually that he had problems separate from hers.

Susan, rated as a woman at moderate risk, had one daughter seven years old. In her first interview, she had been in the program three years and was about to embark on a master's degree in education. Her daughter brought out the best in her—"If I hadn't had my daughter, I could have taken a really bad route. I was depressed, I felt I had nothing to live for, then I felt this person growing inside me and I had a purpose." Initially, Susan was unsure how to be a mother but realized her presence was important for her daughter and they "became attached at the hip." Although her grandmother who had raised her was not an educated person, she emphasized education. Susan does the same with her daughter: "I am really hard on my daughter because I expect her to get straight A's like I did but I try to come to terms with that maybe she's just not that type of person." Susan spoke about her daughter's difficulty in talking and socializing; she knew that it was important that they communicate and that her daughter's own level of achievement be encouraged. Having at first to "pull it out of her," Susan was pleased that her daughter learned to communicate better with her and with other children. Having to cope with her daughter's defiance and rebellion at times, Susan had to overcome her own difficulty with emotional connection. Their struggles made them "a bit closer" because they had to communicate a lot more. At the time of the second interview, after a very difficult year, Susan reported that her daughter's best achievement was her integration and success in her new school. At the beginning of the year, due to her daughter's problems, Susan was terrified and depressed, had trouble sleeping, was extremely unhappy and anxious. She dreaded leaving her daughter at school crying and scared every morning. They had extensive conversations about it and both eventually adjusted. By the end of the year, her daughter had made many friends, and though she experienced academic problems she won an award for outstanding effort and improvement. Susan accepted, even encouraged, her daughter's level of achievement as different from her own. Her growing self-awareness, acceptance of assistance, and her capacity to eventually see her daughter as a separate person reduced her stress level.

Care can have two forms in that "caretaking" and "caring" differ. "Caretaking," as well as providing practical needs, involves doing what is best for or what is in a child's best interests. "Caring" involves expression of caring feelings, that is, caring about another person's well-being. Certainly, these mothers cared about their children and their continual growth. The provision of basic needs—safe shelter, food, education, recreation, etc.—were facilitated by the Project Chance program. Yet the meeting of both the mothers' and children's individual needs involved the capacity to recognize, find, and make use of opportunity to fulfill these needs. A resilient mother could recognize, find, and use what she and her child needed (Jenny lowered her exacting standards and set realistic goals). A restricted mother often required someone to point out alternatives (Julie, who previously had no one to talk with about her trauma and her child's problems, could think about alternatives and consider suggestions in the presence of the interviewer). A mother at moderate risk did well with support (Susan said, "Because there was so much to think about, if I were not helped at Project Chance, I would just have a nervous breakdown"). Being supported herself, she was more able to support the development of her daughter's individuality. A mother at high risk (Vicky) had a much greater struggle. Because of the severe deprivation of her background and premature independence, she knew that besides caring for her children, she had to grow internally (redo herself) before she would be ready for a relationship with a partner.

The capacity to care has multiple and various levels of expression. So too do the characteristics of resilience and autonomy. Clearly, despite differences in expression of caring, resilience, and autonomy, the women's decision to be a mother by giving birth and to care alone was autonomous; seeking and taking the opportunity that the Project Chance program offered demonstrated resilience. Resilience and autonomy appeared to be the underpinnings for the capacity to care in these women and, it does not seem a stretch to say, for all mothers.

# Part III

## Development of mothers alone

*CHAPTER 10*

# Psychodynamic understanding

There are as many psychological approaches to understanding women as mothers and mothering as there are "schools" of psychology. They range from the neuropsychological through the behavioral to the psychodynamic. Because of my own background,[17] I focus on a psychoanalytic understanding which for me is the most coherent of the psychodynamic approaches. I will present briefly some of this theory of women's development and motherhood.

Psychoanalytic theorizing about women's development began, of course, with the "father" of psychoanalysis, Sigmund Freud. Freud initially understood psychosexual development from the boy child's perspective and then he applied this to girls. He proposed that the girl's wish to become a mother is based on envy of the male penis and that the baby

---

[17] Since my training and practice of fifty-plus years, my frames of reference are primarily psychodynamic/analytic; the literature I reference, therefore, is mostly psychoanalytic. Although trained earlier as a social worker (MSW with a clinical psychodynamic approach) and a PhD in psychological research (with a biopsychosocial approach), my understanding of women's development remains psychodynamic/analytic.

represents a symbolic replacement for the imagined lost penis. Freud (1924d) wrote that

> Renunciation of the penis is not tolerated by the girl without some compensation. She slips … from the penis to a baby. Her Oedipus complex[18] culminates in a desire, which is long retained, to receive a baby from her father as a gift—to bear him a child. One has the impression that the Oedipus complex is then gradually given up because this wish is never fulfilled. The two wishes—to possess a penis and a child—remain strongly cathected in the unconscious and help to prepare the female creature for her later sexual role. (pp. 78–79)

Raised and living in a paternalistic society, fatherhood and maleness were of primary interest for Freud. Even his theory of the Oedipus complex was based on a boy's rather than a girl's development (Freud, 1924d). To paraphrase Young-Bruehl (1990), Freud had noted that among the consequences of his theory of a girl's Oedipus complex stemming from the narcissistic wound of not having a penis were a woman's "sense that all women are inferior beings"; that jealousy, as part of her character, stemmed from "penis envy" and that her hostility toward her mother was because her mother had "sent her into the world so insufficiently equipped" (p. 38). Freud began to shift his views on female psychology during his lifetime in step with his growing clinical experience, but psychoanalysis influenced by Freud continued for a long time to maintain that characterologically women develop as passive and receptive; men as active and assertive. Although some early analysts continued to follow Freud's paternalistic thinking about women, many others began to

---

[18] The theory of the Oedipus complex focused on male children and similarly applied to women is understood as follows: A child from three to five years has complex feelings towards parents. Usually, the child has strong love fantasies for the parent of the opposite sex and is rivalrous with the parent of the same sex. Eventually the child realizes that mom and dad have their own private relationship and the child's adult love relationship must be outside the family. The boy gives up his love for mother and identifies with, rather than rivals, father to find his own love. The girl, as an adult in her own right, identifies with mother and gives up her love for father to find her own love (Britton, 1988, paraphrased).

question the notion that a female child's development followed that of a male child and that her primary motivation for motherhood is a wish to have her father's child. A major controversy within the early days of psychoanalysis ensued.

This controversy centered upon the queries: Is a female child psychologically born a woman or does she realize she is a girl and has a female body when she discovers she is not a boy? In the mid-1920s there were two differing theoretical positions: Freud, Helene Deutsch, and Jeanne Lampl-de Groot led the group that maintained that development was essentially masculine and that a girl came to identify as female only when she imagined she lacked a penis; Karen Horney, Ernest Jones, and Otto Fenichel ascribed to the point of view that gender identity (i.e., primary femininity) was an inborn phenomenon. This theoretical controversy continued and then went underground for several decades.

By the mid-1960s psychoanalysts became aware of new research into the biological underpinnings of sexual development and functioning (Stoller, 1964, 1968, 1975). The earlier controversy was reawakened. There followed a resurgence of interest, in the late 1960s and 1970s, in revising Freud's initial theory of female development. By the 1970s many analysts maintained that core gender identity belongs to the first year of life, penis envy is more often to be considered a defensive maneuver,[19] and orgasm as not dependent on emotional maturity. Psychoanalyst Ruth Easser, unconstricted by orthodoxy, prescient of what is generally accepted today, stated, "A woman must feel complete and proud within herself before she can gain pleasure and fulfilment in those other facets (sexuality, procreation, motherhood) of femaleness" (Easser, 1974). In 1976, Gertrude Ticho summarized, "There seems to be little doubt that girls do not want to become men but want to develop into independent autonomous women" (p. 140).

---

[19] In this sense "penis envy" is used symbolically to represent and defend against the painful feelings which ensue when a woman feels inferior to a man or femaleness is inferior to maleness. Various defensive maneuvers occur, such as a woman may consider herself childlike and helpless or alternately, behave in a pseudo-masculine way.

Rosemary Balsam[20] said that, even when training as an analyst, she "could not credit that anyone (*including psychoanalysts*) could think about a girl the way Freud did ... How did his mind work that he accepted as 'truth' a distortion that a girl thought she was first a boy?" (Balsam & Harris, 2012, p. 34). Balsam's comments do not reflect a disrespect for Freud or a negation of his eventual understanding of the significant contribution of mothers to the development to both sons and daughters. As Balsam writes (2012):

> The vast majority of analysts concede that Freud was wrong in his conception of women's psychic development. Nevertheless, about much else he was often right. Freud may have been wrong about the particulars of female development but he understood that bodily experience matters to us, and he offered a brilliant gambit upon which analysts have been building ever since. (p. 3)

The gambit being that "the ego is first and foremost a bodily ego" (Freud, 1923b, p. 24).

Psychoanalysts today have largely moved beyond Freud in elaborating their understanding of female development. It is now generally accepted that a girl's conscious awareness of her female identity occurs from the earliest sense of self—"I am a girl," "I have a girl's body," "I have a vagina, not a penis," and "I can have babies." A little girl first and foremost realizes what she has and what she is uniquely capable of, not what she does not have. Emily, a bright little girl of twenty months, quoted by Mayer, said "Mummy has a bottom ... Emily has a bottom ... Daddy has a bottom ... Mummy has a vulva ... and Emily has a vulva ... but Daddy has something funny in his vulva!" (Mayer, 1985, p. 331). Emily's observations emphasize that little girls are first aware of how they are made before they learn how a boy is made. The concept of primary femininity which "entails an assumption that the girl develops some mental representation of genital femaleness at an early age" (Mayer, 1985, p. 344) gradually developed. It is currently understood by the majority of theorists and clinicians that the development of girls and boys differs

---

[20] Balsam's mother had a feminist spirit; Balsam was a mother herself, and as a psychiatrist and psychoanalyst treated women who had had a baby.

significantly and that the development of motherhood is different than fatherhood.[21]

Freud, in fact, is recognized for his astuteness in separating a woman's sexuality from her capacity to bear children. Later, Freud acknowledged the importance of the mother to a child: "A child's first erotic object is the mother's breast that nourishes it; love has its origin in attachment to the satisfied need for nourishment" (Freud, 1940a, p. 188). Freud, however, emphasized the *child's* relationship to the mother and not the *mother's* relationship to the child (Akhtar, 2012, p. 2). Those after Freud (analysts and others) continued to elucidate the essential role of mother in a child's development.

The acceptance of primary femininity in psychoanalytic thought, however, helped to give the mother–daughter relationship a primary position. Akhtar (2012) noted that "The maternal side of the equation, while hardly separable from that of the child, began to be addressed to a greater extent by Rene Spitz, Donald Winnicott, Margaret Mahler, and John Bowlby. Subsequent analysts added further nuances to the insights provided by these pioneers" (p. 2). For example, Edith Jacobson (1968) maintained that the development of the girl's wish to bear a child, "while not definitely and heterosexually constituted before the Oedipal phase, goes back to a long pregenital history of fixation [*attachment*] to the mother" (p. 523). Here, Jacobson strongly asserts that the development of a woman's wish, married or unmarried, to bear a child is initially based on her attachment to her mother.

By 1998, Kulish and Holtzman had proposed that, instead of the Oedipus myth applicable to boys, the Persephone myth[22] better suits

---

[21] Recognition of one's body as being female or male does not define feelings about core gender identity. There is much more work to be done on the psychoanalytic understanding of feelings about the nature of one's body, and variations expressed in object choice, behavior, role, self-image, and self-presentation.

[22] The Persephone myth involves a mother–daughter relationship and for both the developmental task of separation–individuation. That is, the task of a young girl leaving her mother to become a woman in her own right. Persephone, the daughter is attracted by beautiful flowers to go off from her mother, Demeter. She is lured to the underworld by a powerful man, Hades. Her mother, going through the struggle of losing a child, angrily mourns her daughter. Eventually, her daughter eats "forbidden fruit" (a pomegranate symbolic of sexuality and fertility) and remains with the man returning to visit

women's development as it emphasizes the importance of the mother–daughter relationship. The controversies within female psychology now shifted to the complex process by which girls develop into independent autonomous women. A woman's self-development is separate from the development of her child.

Recently, Balsam (2017) wrote, "Birthing [and breast feeding] is a clearly female body capacity, forever societally fraught with moral judgments about life style, gender role identity, and sexual object choice. This magisterial sign of mature female bodily capacity was never granted full entry into the general psychoanalytic theory of mind ..." (p. 62). She later notes that some analysts have written on aspects of the female body and genital sexuality development, for example, "Raphael-Leff (1993, 2015) ... specifically on infertility, pregnancy, childbirth and childrearing" (Balsam, p. 84), but currently, there is no single overarching theory of female development. Indeed, now many analysts work toward understanding a "nonbinary" (i.e., neither masculine nor feminine), pluralistic (for boys and girls), or transsexual identity rather than the traditional understanding of gender identity or object choice orientation. Much remains to be understood and developed before a contemporary definition of gender, of family, and of lifestyles can be developed within psychoanalytic theory.

It is generally accepted that a woman's ideal psychosexual development as well as her capacity for motherhood are based on caring, supportive relationships with both mother and father, and positive relationships with family members within a facilitating social situation. However, very few of the study women experienced these sorts of positive relationships. As I have noted often, many of the women in the study came from single parent—primarily mother—families. Frequently, physically or emotionally abusive parents had little support or resources to give. Further, many of the study women experienced unstable relationships with their partners. For some, pregnancy was desired and for others it was not a personal decision but unplanned or unwanted and, for a few, forced. Yet, as Daniel Stern asserted, pregnancy becomes the "dominant organizing axis for the mother's psychic life" (Stern, 1995, p. 172). Even without the other usual psychosocial developmental advantages which promote a woman's sense of herself as a person and a mother, the women

---

her mother only a few times a year. Persephone's mother must accept her daughter as an adult woman who has her own life and will visit intermittently.

in my study chose to keep and mother their children. Perhaps Stern's assertion is applicable here. It seems also that besides the "organizing" influence of pregnancy and in spite of difficult family histories, unsatisfying love relationships, and unsupportive social circumstances, other factors can contribute to a woman's development as a resilient, autonomous, and maternal woman.

Among these factors is a woman's degree of identification and disidentification with her own mother or maternal figures. The more a woman could identify with the positive aspects of her maternal figures and disregard or disidentify with the negative qualities, the more secure she felt in developing her own way of mothering. Disidentification and emotional or physical distance from mother do not mean that her birth mother (even if abusive, abandoning, or absent) is not important, or not thought about as a vital person in a woman's life. All of the women spoke with intensity about their mothers more than anyone else in their lives, even when asked a general opening question such as, "Tell me about your family." Some women refused any contact with their mothers, some expressed anger and resentment, others clung to her, some improved their relationship with her, some appreciated any help given, others recognized and were empathetic towards their mother's struggles, some tried to help mother. Even with positively influential mother substitutes, birth mothers remained significant (positively and negatively) in the women's internal world. Perhaps it is this significance that contributed to the women's decision to bear and keep their babies even if it meant doing it differently than their mother and on their own.

My assertions of the effects of identification, disidentification, and modeling on a woman's view of herself as a mother are supported in the psychological literature:

> ... it is through the processes of modeling, identification, and internalization that girls learn how to mother ... regardless of whether the models are positive or negative. In general, good mothering breeds good mothers. ... The negative model of "I will never do what my mother did" can powerfully influence a woman's capacities to mother. ... A woman overcomes a troubled past and escapes the repetition of it by putting into perspective and rendering her earlier experience of being mothered. (Fonagy et al., 1991 in Fallon & Brabender, 2012, p. 17)

The women in my study with the lowest differentiation from their mothers were those few who lived a restricted life, whereas a majority of the three other groups thought of themselves as having achieved separateness. That is, they developed a dependency on themselves and confidence in doing things their "own way."

How do those women with traumatic life circumstances who do not have the support of therapy manage psychologically? Vaillant wrote, "Perhaps Freud's most original contribution to human psychology was his inductive postulation that unconscious 'defense mechanisms' protected the individual from painful emotions, ideas and drives" (1992, p. 3). Denial of the difficulties a mother will face in rearing a child is not uncommon among new mothers, alone or not. Given the elation of giving birth to a child, the potential pleasure and joy of seeing a child grow, most new mothers do not realize the effort needed, the inevitable mixed feelings, and the problems which will come in raising a child. Vaillant noted that "Denial involves the automatic refusal to acknowledge painful or disturbing aspects of inner or outer reality" (1992, p. 272). As noted previously, denial can be an adaptive defense. That is, non-psychotic denial[23] which allows a person to do what has to be done. The best example of "healthy" or necessary denial is that of a soldier who must go into battle and kill the enemy. If the soldier did not deny what killing another person means to him in ordinary circumstances,[24] killing in a war would not be possible. By the same token, although true for most parents, a woman who chooses to mother alone (especially those with few resources or little support) must consciously ignore some of the difficulties she will inevitably face, especially at first, if she is to make the decision. Those who deny adaptively make what they believe to be the "right" decision, without thinking about the difficulties they will face. Although less a defense than an instinct, protection of one's child from danger (most mothers will leap like a lion if her child is threatened) may also contribute to a woman's maternal drive.

---

[23] Psychotic denial is total denial of reality. For example, external reality is denied: "I am not in the hospital; this is my country club" (Vaillant, 1992, p. 272). Severe distortion of thoughts feelings and events can be psychotic.

[24] This statement discounts a characteristically sadistic person who consciously or unconsciously derives pleasure in killing and whose impulse is unleashed in war.

It is possible that the development of "normal" altruism can be a significant characteristic which contributes to the ability of women to sacrifice for their children, particularly if mothering alone. Seelig and Rosof (2001) wrote about various kinds of altruism. Two types apply here: *proto altruism*, being mostly biological and instinctive is hard-wired in the human brain and assists a mother to be protective of her infant; *generative altruism* gives a mother unconflicted pleasure in contributing to a child's successful achievement. The mothers in my study did choose to care for their children and many expressed feelings of pride in their children's success.

Sandler and Sandler (1998) shed some light on how women with emotionally deprived, often destructive backgrounds develop their capacity to mother. To paraphrase, the Sandlers propose that in the absence of the external object (the "good enough" mother), a child can develop in phantasy the wished-for caregiver. That is, there are two kinds of experience: subjective experience and wished-for experience which does not actually occur in reality. Despite deprived histories, persons can develop an internal wish for what is needed emotionally and can find other people and opportunity to fulfill these wishes. Fulfilled wishes create a sense of security and well-being. Further, "Just as relationships to others can be regarded as role relationships, so too are relationships, in thought or phantasy, to the various images in the conscious or unconscious wishes and phantasies deriving from the structures we call 'internal objects'" (Sandler & Sandler, 1998, p. 76). They also note that "Many character traits can be considered to be techniques that the individual has unconsciously developed to evoke specific role responses in others" (p. xiii).

Three examples of the study women support the Sandlers' assertion that internal images contribute to maternal development. Recall low-risk Jenny's ability to mother and high-risk Vicky's process of "redoing" herself. Jenny used both positive and negative identifications to differentiate herself from the negative models of her birth parents and identify with the nurturing care received from foster parents. Vicky realized she did not want to be like her mother and decided she had to better her life. Jenny seemed to have an internal image of how she wished to be mothered and a mother substitute with whom to identify. Vicky had a picture of what a mother ought to be but knew she had to develop herself as a woman before she could mother well. Furthermore, an alumna who experienced severe trauma put in her own words the concept of the development of an internal maternal image even when an external one is lacking:

> My immature alcoholic mother told me that when I was born, she made a vow to hate me but I had one significant teacher who took me under her wing and made me feel OK. Then Project Chance gave me confidence. Someone believed in me. As a member of the board, I was with bright, kind, encouraging women who solicited my opinion. I started to believe in myself.

This woman believed enough in herself to successfully find meaningful work and care for her children. With appropriate and ongoing therapy, she came to terms with her traumatic background and developed her capacity to slowly enter a loving relationship. She also acknowledged that external support helped her build a more self-confident internal image; her increased confidence, intelligence and determination led to autonomy and eventually a reciprocal relationship.

Freud's early observation "we must give up the unfruitful contrast between external and internal factors, between experience and constitution" (1912c, p. 238) must be paid attention to. Certainly, a combination of internal and external factors contributes to a woman's development of her maternal capacity. A woman's internalizations (how she thinks of people and the world) are moderated by individual capacities and revisions over time and then combined with what external circumstances emotionally mean to her. Although relationships with mother, father, and the parental couple are developmentally central,

> the growing child is also affected by his or her relationships with siblings, grandparents, and extended family members. These relationships offer their own psychological benefits, including the potential for ameliorating the deficiencies and disturbances in the child–parent relationship. Step-relatives, non-family members and even animals and ecological surround of the child help him or her grow, express, mentalize and metabolize his or her intrapsychic goings-on. The child's inner dialogue with representations of divine figures also provides an avenue for working out

conflicts and sustaining hope in face of difficult developmental
tasks. (Akhtar, 2005, p. 51)

Furthermore, such relationships and the child's inner conversation with
them influence later choices of friends, partners, work, and interests.

The object relations theorists, primarily psychoanalysts Fairbairn
(1954) and Bowlby (1988), emphasized that developmentally, children's
need for a relationship with others is central. A child initially is motivated
by basic needs (e.g., food, warmth, touch, bodily care, emotional responsiveness) to engage the caregiving person—usually mother. Children
communicate their needs differently according to their inborn character
and mothers respond differently. A child may naturally be active or passive, loud or quiet, happy or upset, angry or cajoling, beautiful or plain,
etc., all attributes which evoke various responses from mother. And a
"good enough" mother tries to be "in tune" with how a child commu-
nicates and tries to understand and fill the need communicated. Other
psychoanalysts and investigators (e.g., Ainsworth et al., 1978; Fonagy
et al., 1991; Main, 1993), through their research have gone on to develop
attachment and mentalization theory and identified patterns of attachment (secure, avoidant, ambivalent, or resistant). This understanding of
attachment patterns was developed through research into clinical and
nonclinical, child and adult populations and has led to the design of
measurements for further study in both populations. Adopted theoreti-
cally and clinically by psychoanalysts, attachment theory is influential
in other psychological theory as well. Numerous other studies provide
evidence of the buffering effect of social support and of opportunity to
ameliorate distress. Internally these buffers add to a mother's sense of
hope, increase her dignity, and decrease her sense of helplessness and
shame. The "right kind of support" decreases her distress and increases
her sense of worthiness to receive help.

Although it is generally accepted that good enough parents or parent substitutes, personal attributes such as intelligence, and adequate
resources contribute to a maternal capacity, these fortunate life circumstances do not always prevent symptoms of distress. It is well known that
although no family is perfect, children from relatively loving families
can have emotional problems. Clinical observations especially allow us
to observe that many women are good mothers and yet they, even those

with partners and/or material resources, can suffer from emotional problems. Conversely, unfortunate life circumstances do not always lead to emotional problems.

In summary, this brief outline of relevant psychoanalytic theory has highlighted my understanding, as a psychoanalyst, of women's development and relevant factors (secure family relationships, positive life experiences, and personal characteristics) which can contribute to a capacity to mother, even to mother alone. I have also queried and attempted, with examples of women mothering alone, to answer whether and how women who experience unfortunate life circumstances (loss, deprivation, abuse) can develop maternal capacity. The next chapter will discuss the "right kind of support" based on their strengths and limitations and consider society's role in providing for women mothering alone the opportunity to become successful mothers and raise healthy children—the opportunity and support to better their lives.

## CHAPTER 11

# Society's role

During the last century or so, there have been significant societal changes in attitudes towards women mothering alone. In brief, with less condemnation of sexuality and more opportunity to raise children alone, there is more acceptance of sole-support mothers regardless of marital status. The repercussions for their children are also much less negative. There is, as well, considerable recognition that it is best for children to remain with their birth mothers and for women not to be forced to place their babies for adoption. Moreover, if women, alone or not, are to be successful mothers who raise healthy children, they need adequate resources. Practical resources for mothers with children include good secure housing, adequate food and finances, education, child care, medical services (both physical and psychological), transportation; emotionally, they need supportive, understanding relationships, time and places for rest and relaxation, as well as intellectual stimulation. Of course, such ideal resources are needed by all mothers but especially by those who are mothering alone.

Women mothering alone who have their own resources, and the physical and emotional ability to use them, are best able to raise their children. Recall the literary and clinical examples (Clara, Dori, Camilla, and Gwen) described in previous chapters. The focus here, however, has been on the small group of women in my study who were without the necessary resources. For them to raise physically and emotionally healthy children, they required society's help. For these fifty-eight women necessary resources came from Project Chance, supported by both government and private philanthropy. These resources allowed them to take advantage of the opportunity for post-secondary education. Interviewing these women stimulated not only my interest in how they fared within such a program but also sparked a broader interest in the needs of the many disadvantaged women mothering alone. What I learned from the mothers in this small study highlights what could be accomplished more broadly if societal resources could be mobilized.

Society's role begins with awareness and acceptance of the extent of the social problem—that in our wealthy Western societies there are many women mothering alone who do not have adequate resources for themselves and their children. Secure, sufficient housing is of prime importance. Along with housing is the need for income sufficient to provide basic needs and for enough education to obtain work. Without adequate housing, income and child care assistance, access to further education is extremely difficult, if not next to impossible. This reality is vividly exemplified by Camila[25] in *This Is All I Got* (L. Sandler, 2020). After an exhaustive search but unable to find housing and being asked to leave a shelter, she could not continue her education:

> Two weeks into the new quarter and Camila was already exhausted. Two weeks of putting Alonso to bed in his bouncer at eight o'clock, taking a nap, waking to feed him two hours later, and putting him back to sleep in her bed, before she could sit down at her desk and do her homework. At school that morning, Camila had heard the dean's list for the second quarter was hanging on the wall outside the provost's closed office door. She walked by to check it out. There, listed right at the top, was her name. She was too tired to feel achievement. (L. Sandler, 2020, p. 220)

---

[25]The woman in *This Is All I Got* happens to have almost the same name Camila as the woman in the autobiography *this is happy* (Camilla Gibb, 2015). However, their names are spelt differently—Gibb's with two 'lls' and the other with one 'l'. They also sound different when spoken.

Camila stopped university to look for whatever work she could get to support herself and her child.

Further education does not necessarily mean attending college or university. Many women mothering alone have not completed high school; for these, most often teenage mothers, further education can mean completing high school. In fact, the need to complete high school has been given more recognition than the need for post-secondary education or training. One woman related that she had gone back to complete high school when she was pregnant, and after giving birth, was allowed to bring her baby to class and to breastfeed as needed. Later she went on to post-secondary education thanks to Project Chance. Another said, "I don't believe people should live mediocre lives when they can educate themselves. No way I was having a child without at least high school so I went back to school during my first pregnancy, it was my responsibility." She too continued post-secondary education with Project Chance. Opportunities for both high school[26] and post-secondary education are desirable for sole-support mothers. For university, a woman needs intelligence, motivation, and good work habits to achieve a degree. However, university does not suit all; further training at a community college, a trade school, or an apprenticeship could be what some women want after high school. Furthermore, a university degree may be less suitable preparation for reasonably paid work than training in other work areas. Nor does further education always lead to suitable and adequately paid work. Canadian Supreme Court Justice, the Honorable Rosalie Abella—the mother of employment equity—commented that women's "ability to choose [work] is often illusory when they bear the majority of household responsibilities" (Fine, 2021, p. 16). This is particularly true for women who alone are responsible for children, finances, and household.

The Employment Equity Act was adopted in Canada in 1986 and revised in 1995 and is now influential world-wide.

> The purpose of this Act is to achieve equality in the workplace so that no person shall be denied employment opportunities or benefits for reasons unrelated to ability and, in the fulfillment of

---

[26] There seem to be more opportunities for pregnant teens to continue high school than for older mothers alone to pursue post-secondary education.

that goal, to correct the conditions of disadvantage in employment experienced by women ... by giving effect to the principle
that employment equity means more than treating persons in the
same way but also requires special measures and the accommodation of differences.[27]

Employment equity should not be confused with pay equity. Employment
equity aims to increase the number of women in well-paid occupations.
In contrast, pay equity implicitly recognizes how difficult it is for women
to integrate into predominantly male occupations, and instead aims to
increase the pay of predominantly female occupations. Employment equity
also addresses the situation of aboriginal people, visible minorities, and
people with disabilities, whereas pay equity addresses solely the dilemma
that predominantly female occupations tend to be underpaid. Frequently,
women have been discriminated against not only because of their gender
but also because they are members of one or more of the other minorities.
Many sole-support mothers need not only equal opportunity for work
with decent pay but often work accommodation—for example, time off
when a child is ill or when meetings with teachers must be attended. Such
opportunity and accommodation result not only from society's acceptance that vulnerable members have real needs but from substantive laws,
government legislation, and effective means of enforcement.

Housing, education, work, and income alone are not enough, as one
woman, previously quoted, commented:

> Housing and a good education don't mean anything, if in your
> house, you don't have the basic education of how to be! How am
> I supposed to be as a mother? Who am I supposed to be? I don't
> know that.

This plea is especially meaningful to those women whose mothers or
their substitutes did not provide a "good enough" model. Can women
learn "how to be" from other than mothers? Can support come from
other substitutes? The answer to this question of substitutes is yes,
as seen from this study.

---

[27] This information was found on the internet under Employment Equity Act in Canada.

Certainly, social support is important for all people—we are social human beings—but social support is an absolute necessity for women mothering alone. They do not have the support of a spouse and are mostly without helpful family relationships. One woman said,

> Project Chance was the difference between life and death. I did not have strong ties with the other women but I knew I wasn't alone. We all struggled to do something good, even if we were at different levels of the struggle.

The mothers felt supported to know that there were others in the same situation. Many participated in the parenting group and found being with other mothers helpful. Yet living with other women was not without difficulty. Gossip, criticism, uneven involvement in common responsibilities, and variations in need for company contributed. The relational skills of the administration and staff often but not always facilitated a positive atmosphere. Aspects of the program such as the parenting group were helpful to some and not others, especially if the majority of women in the group had children in an age group different from their child's age. Each woman had to find the person or group which best related to her needs. Interestingly, many found the friendly janitor's helpfulness provided consistent support.

A confidant, readily available, who offers a relationship with reciprocal confidences gives the most personal support. A mother's capacity and need for one or more confidant(e)s varies greatly: Some have the capacity for and the availability of a confidant and confide as needed; others prefer to keep their privacy and may or may not have the ability to enter a confiding relationship; still others, especially when under stress, may need a great deal of support. Some of the study women at moderate risk claimed to have many confidants and I wondered about the depth of these relationships; a person rarely has more than a few people with whom one can confide the most personal problems, who are readily available and reciprocally confide. To provide the "right kind of support" each of these variations in the women needs to be understood and respected. This was reinforced for me when one woman, needing to keep her privacy, was not very forthcoming in her first interview and could not make herself available for the second. For her, support involved respect for her restricted lifestyle. However, most mothers alone need to tell their story and only very few residents (four out of forty-four) refused to participate in the study. The majority of participants who kept their appointments spoke with me willingly. They wanted their stories heard. The minimal support of the opportunity to tell their stories in the interviews seemed important to them. Listening as they spoke openly about their situations and backgrounds, hearing a year or so later what they remembered from their first interview, led me to realize that being heard was of significant value to these mothers. When I thanked one woman for her time, she said, "You don't know what you have done for me. Just being able to verbalize this felt so good."[28]

Health care services, both physical and psychological, provided in timely and appropriate ways, are especially essential for those mothers and their children who had physical or emotional problems. A small group of the women and children had a need for medical help which was usually available under Canada's national health care system. At times a few mothers found it difficult to find the right doctor for themselves or their children. A greater problem is access to quality mental health services due to high cost and insurance limits. The most difficult part for me as a psychoanalyst, accustomed to listening for emotional problems and in a position to offer help, was realizing that my role as a researcher was to interview the women, not to engage in therapy. What made this particularly difficult was that the women recognized their own need for therapy but could not afford it—"I loved therapy but couldn't afford to continue," or "I have a mood disorder and see a psychiatrist infrequently but there is no time to talk further," or "I needed ten years of counseling but could afford it only after I graduated and had work." Psychotherapy, conducted by qualified therapists who do not have medical degrees, is covered only minimally through private insurance plans (at least in Canada and the US).

There is no doubt that a limited program such as Project Chance can be helpful to only a small number of sole-support mothers who require assistance. Certainly, the women had to fulfill certain requirements to

---

[28] I knew it felt good to have one's story listened to by an attentive listener; even one session can be helpful. However, as a therapist, I realized that many of these women could use further help but, as an interviewer, I was limited in what I could offer.

be admitted and continue in the program: For example, they had to be enrolled and remain in a post-secondary program; they had to find resources to pay a portion of their subsidised rent, usually by obtaining scholarships or summer work. They shared responsibility for the care of the residence. Characteristics for fulfilling these requirements were the capacities for involvement, responsibility, and accountability. Meeting these requirements, which was not always easy, enabled the women to achieve their educational goals while raising their children.

Is it possible for society to meet the needs of the many, many women mothering alone without resources who are not in a program such as Project Chance? How can they be helped to improve their own and their children's lives? Before a society can develop ways of providing even these basic needs of women mothering alone, a caveat is required. It is generally accepted that wealthy countries have an obligation to provide assistance to the many who live in underprivileged circumstances and have numerous unmet needs. To meet this obligation, governments have developed programs such as social assistance, social security, unemployment benefits, universal health care, low-cost housing, long-term care homes, shelters, food banks, etc. It is also well recognized that such programs go only so far in meeting the basic needs of the neediest of our societies. Certainly, this is a topic well beyond the scope of this book. Women who mother alone are only one group among the many disadvantaged members of society. As I have stressed, the education of women allows them to improve their own lives and also their children's lives. For success in the pursuit of education, however, basic needs must be met.

Program Chance[29] offers a program which allows women the opportunity to pursue their education beyond high school. My study clearly indicates that the vast majority of these mothers and their children

---

[29] To my knowledge only one other comprehensive program (Homeward Bound), which offers opportunity for post-secondary education to sole-support mothers, was developed in Canada well after Project Chance and is discussed in the Afterword. None was found in the United States, the UK, or the Republic of Ireland.

In Israel in 2006, following a six-year-long battle, the nonprofit organization YEDID in conjunction with MK Yuri Stern, the Directorate of the Single Parent Families Project in the Ministry of Industry Commerce and Employment and with Treasury funding began a special project. Single mothers will receive supplementary, guaranteed income from the government to be able to study at university. They will also be given stipends

benefited from their time at Project Chance. They are a fortunate group; they had help in meeting their basic needs (above all, housing) which allowed them to pursue their educational goals. As Mathew Desmond, the Pulitzer Prize-winning author of *Evicted*, once told an interviewer, "Without stable shelter, everything else falls apart."[30] Everything does fall apart for the central character, Camila, in *This Is All I Got*. She had to stop her education, take a low paying job just so she and her child could survive. This tragedy is all too common for many underprivileged mothers despite intelligence, determination, and persistence as well as other qualities which they have, like Camila: "… she was a woman who was hellbent on propelling herself out of this shelter, away from the circumstances of her past, toward something solid, ambitious" (L. Sandler, 2020, p. xiv).

The Project Chance program underlines the primary importance of available, affordable, safe, and suitable housing. However, two problems become evident. First, when the women completed the allotted number of years in the program and graduated, they were ready to seek work but first had to find housing. Few could find work immediately, nor did many have adequate finances to tide them over. Many had debts. They needed a transition program that would prepare them for the difficulties they would have to face until they could find housing and work. Regrettably, there was no such program! Second, in 2019, one of the Project Chance residences had to close due to lack of money for needed upkeep. A broken heating system and mold in the apartments forced the closing. The women and children had to find new low-cost housing but even though the women had received notice several months before, persistent search did not lead to new affordable housing at a rent that would allow them to keep their governmental subsidies. A number of the women had to give up their subsidies, seek higher cost housing, and find ways of paying the rent. It is uncertain whether the women who did so were able to continue their education. The situation highlights

for living expenses equivalent to the subsidy they had been receiving (www.yedid.org.il/english/NewsMain.asp?id =596).
[30] Desmond, M. *Evicted* in *New York Times* book review May 10, 2020, p. 10.

the problems of bureaucratic misinformation or lack of attention and government inaction.[31]

The immense difficulties that single mothers without resources face has been underlined in the Netflix series based on S. Land's 2019 memoir, *Maid*. The story is told of the will of Alex, a young mother, to survive through hard work, low pay, and abuse while squelching her intelligence, her abilities.

> … as *Maid* shows us, a life without means or support is like trying to build a Jenga tower on a tilting table. One missed bus, one sniffle that keeps Alex's daughter out of daycare, one late rent payment and the whole thing tumbles down. For Alex, every day is pulse-pounding, because she's in a perpetual race against imminent disaster. (Schneller, *Globe and Mail*, October 6, 2021)

After much self-sacrifice, shame, and seemingly impossible dreams for a better life she uses her determination and ability to write; she writes about her experience.

A few other mothers, who have had housing assistance but lose it, still manage (again, due to extraordinary self-sacrifice) to improve if not their own lives, the lives of their children. For example, one mother tells her story of eviction and how she managed to assist her teenage daughter's success: "On a frigid New Year's Eve my teenage daughter and I, along with our two cats, became homeless" (Rabideau, 2019). She recalled that she had been taught that the children of single parents were less likely to graduate even from high school, and were prone to teen pregnancy, drugs, and alcohol. She set about disproving this prediction. Living on low income, multiple jobs, and sacrificing possessions, she offered her daughter love and determination. Her biracial daughter, facing bullying at school, focused on academic achievement, eventually attended on scholarship, and graduated from a prestigious university.

My conviction endures: In extremely difficult circumstances women mothering alone can do extraordinary things given the right kind of support.

---

[31] See the *CBC News* article, posted on Google under Project Chance, November 6, 2019.

As emphasized by my study, opportunity for further education is one example of the right kind of support. A touching letter written by a Project Chance resident highlights that this kind of opportunity is the right kind of support:[32]

Dear Friends of Project Chance,

> I moved into Project Chance after a very difficult year as a full-time student and single parent. Soaring rent costs required me to work many hours which had a direct effect on my academic performance. I had lots of hope and energy for my future but I was faced with impending failure.

> I sought help at the local social service, which suggested Project Chance. Right away, I applied, was accepted and moved in a few months later. It truly felt like I had won the jackpot at the lottery.

> Since then, lots of changes have happened in my life. I can now afford my rent and I have enough money left for groceries, bills, books and tuition. My daughter and I have finally left an isolated existence and we are now part of a dynamic community of moms and children who were in similar situations.

> Today, my daughter has her own bedroom and a safe backyard to play in, and I have lots more time for her and my studies. A social worker is available when we need help with community resources or when the stress becomes overwhelming. Parenting classes are also available for us and they are just the best.

> My daughter recently began at a specialized school and she has the chance of attending an after-school program in our building, thereby reducing the time she spends in an institutionalized setting. Better yet, she is surrounded by people who love her.

> Project Chance wants single mothers to achieve their academic goals without sacrificing the welfare of their children. And they are very

---

[32] This spontaneous letter was circulated to raise funds and is public information. Any identifying information has been disguised.

good at this. Your donations help us make our dreams come true and allow us to break free from an endless cycle of poverty.

I have now finished my studies at college in literature and am about to embark in the literature program at university. Working in the literary field has been my ambition since I was five years old. But without Project Chance, my goals would have been impossible.

Thank you so much for transforming my dream into a reality.

It takes more than opportunity for mothers alone to succeed. Mothers who improve their lives while alone have the inner strength of a self image which includes imagination, determination, and persistence to reach a goal as well as the availability and acceptance of support. My study documents that these characteristics were present in the underprivileged women of Project Chance. Other women who possess these characteristics, but without resources and available opportunity, can sometimes make opportunity for themselves. A woman of mixed race, who as a foster child lived at thirty-six addresses, became pregnant as a teen, survived a terrible beating by the child's father, after which she became determined to change her life. While mothering her child and with only a grade 7 education, eventually through gargantuan effort she completed academic requirements for a degree to work in child welfare and eventually entered law school. After her first year, she nearly quit but with the persuasion and support of a professor who stood by her throughout, she graduated as a lawyer (MacDonald, 2019. p. A1). Women with such inner fortitude are rare; most need society's assistance; all, with fortitude or not, need personal support.

It is true that a woman's ability to succeed depends on what is within her as well as what is around her. Many mothers and children have inadequate housing or have had to leave their homes with nowhere to go. Many must live in shelters at the expense of a government. They often have little education, unsatisfying work if any at all, inadequate income, insufficient support, underdeveloped determination, and likely are unable to change their situation. With education and satisfying, well-paid work, they are less of a burden to society as they support themselves and their family. Additionally, one of the most profound fears of any mother is, "If something happens to me, who will take care of my children?"

For a single parent, this fear is even greater—they know that "Without me, my children will not have a parent." The support of families and friends can somewhat alleviate a mother's greatest fear but for women with little support, more responsibility falls on society's contribution.

What, then, is society's role? It is huge. My study of fifty-eight women in Project Chance demonstrated how helpful a program focused on higher education can be to disadvantaged women mothering alone. But there are so few such programs, even in wealthy countries. Less pejorative attitudes, less blame on have-nots, greater recognition of need, even awareness of the extent of the problem—the increasing numbers of children with one parent—are essential aspects of change but they are not enough. Real change is brought about by meaningful action. Such action can begin with individuals, with group pressure, with persistent publicity. In addition, society must find a way to mobilize government funding and private philanthropy to multiply programs such as Project Chance as well as other kinds of facilitating programs. When we improve the lives of women mothering alone and their children, society benefits by their contributions to the common good.

## CHAPTER 12

# Afterword

"**A** Plea for Opportunity," the subtitle of this book, suggests what women mothering alone need if they are to better their own and their children's lives. They need "opportunity"! What kind of opportunity do they require to meet their needs? The study of the intelligent underprivileged women in Project Chance, all of whom are in a program which provides opportunity for post-secondary education, provides some answers to these questions. What was learned?

To begin, while there has been an increase in the number of women mothering children on their own, especially in the last fifty years, there has also been a positive shift in societal acceptance of their situation. At the same time, especially in Western societies, there has been some small recognition of society's responsibility to assist those less fortunate in achieving their potential to fulfil their life tasks. Mothering is indeed a major life task with multiple components. Mothering is more than just giving birth and fulfilling childcare tasks. A woman "becomes a mother" when she develops qualities which promote her ability to raise her children so that they are able to grow and develop their potential. Development of these maternal qualities requires both personal growth and social change. Personal growth includes individual abilities and potential. Social change includes not only changes in attitudes but also provision of opportunity. These thoughts about mothering and change apply, of course, to all women with children, but this book focuses on women alone with children who have had less than adequate parenting, have very few resources, especially financial and, on their own, are unable to pursue the further education they seek.

The women in my study taught much about the identification and growth of these maternal qualities through their openness and generosity. Obviously, intelligence at a high enough level for their acceptance to post-secondary education is assumed for all the study women. But it takes more than intelligence to access opportunity and succeed. Once having made the choice to mother a child—a commitment for at least eighteen years—other characteristics and strategies are required. Determination is essential if a woman is to mother her children and study at the same time—for example, enter a college or university program that is suitable to her intelligence, ability, and interests. Determination is enhanced by three other characteristics: resilience, autonomy, and caring, discussed previously.[33] All are essential for any woman becoming a mother. With good enough parenting which tends to facilitate a strong, supportive internalized model of a mother, most women develop these characteristics. Given adequate resources, they are able to mother their children and develop themselves as women. What was learned here about becoming a mother alone is based on some ninety interviews with fifty-eight women with disadvantaged backgrounds, all of whom are fortunate to have been accepted in a program which provides opportunity with the necessary support for post-secondary education. This, admittedly, is a limited sample of women who are currently in the program, or have graduated from a unique-at-the-time comprehensive program which facilitated their post-secondary education. Though the findings are not generalizable, they do provide some insight into the plight and needs of many mothers alone.

Though being a single parent, even with adequate resources, requires double duty, it is especially difficult for those women who themselves have not had good enough parents. Yet, the study women with disadvantaged

---

[33] See Chapters 7, 8, and 9.

backgrounds and much less than adequate parenting revealed several ways through which they could "become a mother." Some already had an internalized model of a good enough mother, perhaps for some, their own birth mother. Others were able to find a substitute, someone other than their own mother with whom they could identify. Women who lacked that "someone" found the strength within themselves to imagine the kind of mother they wanted to be. Even those few among the Project Chance alumni who, due to personal difficulties, had been unable to complete their post-secondary education recalled what they had learned in the program to shore up their mothering capacities.

An internalized model of motherhood does not mean that a woman becomes a carbon copy of a model or swallows whole what she experiences, sees, reads, or is told about mothering. To paraphrase Winnicott,[34] mothers who are told what to do, or read it in a book can lose touch. They can feel incompetent and fail to act in a timely intuitive way. That is, a woman must be able to trust her intuition—what the right kind of mothering is for her.

As I have emphasized previously, a woman as a mother identifies with the positive aspects of her own mother or of that "someone" or image and disidentifies with negative aspects. She then is able to be creative—to mother in the way that she feels is right for her and her child. Disidentification has been defined as a "term used to describe the shedding of the effects of an erstwhile identification ... implies change in the subjective experience and overt behaviour that emulated a particular object" (*person*) (Akhtar, 2009, p. 81). All of us, women and men, retain an attachment to our birth mother; but the quality of our experience with our mother determines the degree to which we want to be like her or not. For example: when some mothers encourage an idealized attachment, a woman can become overly identified and her mothering creativity is inhibited; others experience a distant or absent mother and can feel angry, alone, and helpless. Those who find a way to mother that works for them have selected their identifications and disidentifications. Even women from intact families and with resources can experience attachment problems that can interfere with their own way

---

[34] Apt quotes attributed to Winnicott were found on the internet under Winnicott quotes.

of mothering. For a woman alone, becoming a mother requires extra strength and determination to develop essential mothering characteristics. To "become a mother" in her own way, especially if from a deprived background, a woman with children requires the right kind of support if she is to succeed in mothering.

As became evident in this study, the "right kind of support" varies from woman to woman. Those with internalized support are quite autonomous in managing life stress and need assistance only when they ask for it; those with restricted lives remain quite attached to their mothers and/or keep stress and the need for outside support to a minimum; whereas others—the majority of the study women—require increased support from multiple sources when their life stress increases; and those with overwhelming life stress and little support are highly vulnerable and require specific intervention. The right kind of support if not from one's own parents comes from parental models wherever found. For example, the right support can come from confidants, friends, and society, including people such as teachers, ministers, counselors, and therapists. To be effective, support from other people requires their being in tune with the woman as an individual—her strengths, her limits, her resources, her child(ren)'s needs, and her needs at this particular time in her life. The women of Project Chance learned about the program through many different supportive people. These people recognized the women's wish for further education and pointed them in the right direction. The women, having already chosen to mother their child and better their lives, took it from there. They had chosen their field of study and did what the application process required. After graduation from high school, they had to enroll in a full-time further education program. Although most were enrolled in university, some even in post-graduate or professional programs, other types of post-secondary education met the Project Chance requirements. Most chose programs which would lead to work with better income.

The opportunity for education is essential but it is not enough. As has been made most clear by the study women, those who are alone must work and study and mother at the same time. Adequate income for mothers alone is their first need, and most often appropriate education is required for work that provides sufficient income. Mothers who are studying and are without independent income need more than opportunity; they need affordable furnished housing, food, tuition, books, clothing, medical/dental care, schooling, and supplies for their children, some of whom have special needs from after-school programs and babysitters. They also need sufficient income for these necessities which often comes through intermittent work, government grants, and student loans, as well as assistance with how to manage loans and debts.

A survey of government assistance in the US, UK, and Canada revealed programs which only partially met these needs. In a search for programs for single mothers, in all three countries, only one other comprehensive program could be found in Toronto. Homeward Bound, which was founded in 2004 (well after Project Chance, which had been founded in 1989), provided many of the essential needs of single mothers and their children. Rather than focusing on opportunity for post-secondary education, the Homeward Bound program concentrated on assisting inadequately housed or homeless mothers to earn diplomas, gain employment, and achieve self-sufficiency. Both of these programs are effective: of the eighteen alumni women in the Project Chance study, sixteen had graduated and found work which they felt provided adequate income and two were still students; a 2017 study of Homeward Bound revealed a similar graduation and work success rate. The Homeward Bound program went somewhat further than Project Chance in that it also provided some access to psychotherapy and family counseling. A much-needed transition program had been developed for when the women, after completing their education, had to repay student debt, and seek work and personal housing. Our wealthy societies should provide many more such comprehensive programs which are needed for women of all underprivileged groups.

This plea for readily available, comprehensive programs does not suggest that all of the difficulties faced by a woman mothering alone would be resolved. Much depends on the capacities and individual strengths of each woman. Miriam Toews, award winning Canadian author, illustrates this truism poignantly in her two most recent novels: *Women Talking* (2018) and *Fight Night* (2021). In the first, a group of essentially illiterate women of varying ages talk with difficulty and at length about the abuse they have received. They then make a courageous decision. Taking their daughters and younger children, they leave their communities, their abusive men, their male leaders, not knowing what they will face in a life outside of what they have known. In *Fight Night*, Toews pays tribute to her own grandmother's and mother's resilience in the face of unbearable heartbreak. An ill, aging, but feisty grandmother, an actor and pregnant mother, and a nine-year-old girl, without a father, live together, on their own. Having been expelled from school for fighting, the girl narrates in a letter to her father the story of the three and the hardships they face. In each of these two novels, the reader does not know how the women will fare in the future or if they are well enough equipped. Yet, these women support each other through severe difficulties and they believe in themselves. These women and girls, similar to the mothers of Project Chance, have the inner strength which contributes to resilience, autonomy, and the capacity to care.

As UNESCO endorses, education and self-sufficiency are essential for all women: "Education is a human right and an essential tool for achieving the goals of equality, development and peace" (UNESCO Report, 2005). Our Western societies have the resources; what is needed further is the social and political will, followed by meaningful action.

As Erna Furman (2001), a highly experienced child analyst and parenting advisor, wrote: "Motherhood is indeed a deeply disconcerting part of our emotional lives—tempting, threatening, enviable, abhorrent, gratifying, exasperating—everywhere, always. It helps to recognize it for what it is, in all its richly textured, uncontained complexity." Furman also quoted Winnicott's 1957 view with which she (and I) agreed: "When even a single man or woman can acknowledge, accept and lend support to all that being and having a mother entail, it helps to make our families, societies and work a safer, kinder place to live in" (p. 219).

It is my hope that this book will awaken for others awareness of the hopes, dreams, goals, strengths, and needs of the many women now mothering alone who lack adequate resources to pursue education, satisfying work, and self-sufficiency, so as to better their own and their children's lives.

# Appendix I

The story of my own mother, I realized later, must also have contributed to my interest in women mothering alone. At age twenty-seven she was left to raise three children, the eldest (myself) three years old, a son of eleven and a half months, and a daughter four months old. My mother was almost eight months pregnant when her husband, in the Canadian army, was posted to Europe in May 1944. Having given birth in June, she was informed in October of his death in battle in Holland.

My mother's educational and work history is relevant: Due to lack of financial resources, at age sixteen, she had left university after one year to pursue teachers' training at "Normal School." Qualifying, but unable to find employment as a teacher in the 1930s, she became a librarian. Once married she gave up work, as expected at the time, to be supported by her husband and have babies. Meanwhile, she pursued her university degree part time and graduated within three years, while giving birth to three children. After her husband's death, she raised her children on a war widow's pension until they were of school age. Then she supplemented her pension with supply teaching. Eventually she worked full time as a school librarian and taught English to commercial students. With the encouragement of her principal, she qualified as a high school teacher.

Then, until retirement, she taught senior year English and finally had the English prize at her school named in her honor. She did not remarry until her children were adults and living their own lives. As children we were fully aware of who my father was and what he was like as a person. My mother often spoke of him, of what had happened to him, where he was buried. My father's siblings (three brothers and four sisters) vividly remembered him to my family. A visit to his grave in Holland where he died, meeting the Dutch family who cared for his grave and kept in touch with my mother, made his sacrifice and our loss more meaningful.

The support of my parents' extended families, the Dutch family assigned to my father's grave, my mother's education and work, her religion and its community, and the necessity of providing for three small children allowed my mother to function well, despite multiple life losses. For her, the loss of her husband compounded much earlier losses (at twenty months, her mother died due to the 1919 flu epidemic two days after giving birth to my aunt; her father, leaving his two daughters to be raised by maternal grandparents, lived at a distance; at age fourteen, her twelve-year-old sister died; and in her late teens, her grandparents who had raised them died). The sustaining memory of warm, caring, secure parenting she had received from her grandparents provided my mother with internalized support.

# Appendix II

## Residence Project Chance Inc.: Program Outcome Study: Contributors to Mother Child Development[35]

This study of the opportunity for post-secondary education provided by "Project Chance" was funded through the Chagnon Foundation.[36]

Fifty-eight women mothering alone[37] were involved; forty of the forty-three residents agreed to participate, giving a participation rate of 93 percent. All of the eighteen alumni whom it was possible to contact responded. Although this was the only alumni sample available due to lack of current contact information, there is some evidence based on graduation status (education completed to graduation or not) that the eighteen participants who were no longer in the program might be

---

[35] This summary of the research project and its findings is based on the O'Neil et al., 2008 report to the Chagnon Foundation which is cited in the references.

[36] The Chagnon Foundation (Fondation Lucie et André Chagnon, at the time, was Canada's largest granting foundation) stimulated and supported financially the research project, "Program Outcome Study: Contributors to Mother Child Development."

[37] Forty-three women had apartments in two different residences—twenty in the first and twenty-three in the second, established several years after the first. Eighteen were alumni.

representative of the total number of alumni. Of the forty residents interviewed, thirty-five agreed to a second interview (return rate 87 percent). This second interview was to determine from the current residents which aspects of the program were helpful and what was lacking. The eighteen alumni were not interviewed a second time as their first interview was focused on the impact of the program on their subsequent lives and the contributions of the program on their ability to provide for themselves and their children. Ninety-three interviews are available to tell the stories of these women mothering alone. Their stories provided the stimulus for this book.

The women residents, mostly in the young adult phase of development, ranged in age from their early twenties to their early thirties; the majority had one child while about one-fourth had two children. Many had never married; 23 percent were separated or divorced. It was possible for them to stay in residence up to five years with an average length of stay being three to four years. The majority were Canadian born, though many had one or more parent born outside of Canada. Sixty-two percent were completing their university degrees with the remainder working on diplomas at a community college. Their programs of study included law, dentistry, social work/counseling, nursing, business, and arts. The first language of 90 percent of the women was English, but a full 60 percent were fluently bilingual and 40 percent could function passably in both French and English. A smaller number of the women spoke at least one third language.

Financial difficulties caused the greatest stress. All of the women were financially strapped. Prior to coming into the program, the women were living on very low incomes comprised of combinations of family allowance, unemployment insurance, part-time work, or loans and bursaries. Disturbingly, 58 percent had existed on income below the poverty line for families living in a large city with one or two children. A small number gave up full-time work to return to school. Their financial situations improved somewhat while in the program, especially with lower cost housing and assistance with child care, but they still had to exert considerable effort to make ends meet.

The fifty-four children currently at Project Chance had been living with their mothers in difficult circumstances. The gender of the children whose mothers were in the study was almost equal (twenty-six sons and twenty-three daughters). Approximately one quarter of the children were reported to have serious physical or emotional problems, adding to the mothers' stress.

Most concerning was the finding that 78 percent of fathers had no or little involvement with their children. That is, 83 percent of the boys and 60 percent of the girls did not have a relationship with their fathers. Only 5 percent of fathers provided even minimal financial support. Lack of available support, even from parents, was also common and increased the women's stress levels.

Prior to being in the program the alumni were similar with regard to their demographics (ethnic background, language proficiency, and their life circumstances). The eighteen alumni had a total of thirty-six children at the time they were interviewed. They also had had similar stress issues. Of the eighteen alumni (age range twenty-six to forty-four), fourteen graduated before leaving the program, two graduated after leaving, and two did not graduate. Of those who graduated, 72 percent completed a university degree and the remainder completed community college. Of the two who did not graduate at all, one left due to depression but later found work after qualifying as a registered nursing assistant; she raised five children on her own. Another woman could not complete her education due to mental illness but supported her children as a skilled laborer. Two other women left for positive reasons: marriage or no longer needing subsidized housing; both of them completed their education later and found work. Fewer than one third of the alumni were with a partner and one third had three or more children. Seventy-seven percent of the alumni provided the sole financial support of their children. The income of the women had improved, for many significantly. The alumni women emphasized that their education and the program increased their self-esteem and made them able to provide for their children even if their income was not yet adequate.

This study considered the women's psychological and physical well-being, the life circumstances which put them at risk, and the kind of support they needed to complete their educational goals and maternal aspirations. Almost half of the women had low rates of depression and anxiety and were without general health problems. The rates of clinical depression and/or symptoms of anxiety or depression were in keeping with rates in young adults which are similar to rates in the general population (O'Neil et al., 2008, p. 19). It was somewhat surprising that only about 20 percent of these student mothers rated themselves as being almost always tired given the energy required for their dual responsibilities (raising children and studying), perhaps suggesting a high degree of determination. They could not afford to allow themselves to be tired. The mean number of stressful life events was approximately ten different events over a two-year period, which is not an unusual rate. What was of more concern is that one third had experienced two or more significant losses during this period. This was a significantly higher number of losses when compared with a population of similar age.

The higher a woman's burden of stressful life events, the greater her symptoms of distress. A woman who had no confidant[38] was at increased risk for four times as many distress symptoms. Secure attachments[39] predicted significantly fewer symptoms whereas distress symptoms were higher for those with insecure attachments.[40]

This project included the women's assessment of the helpful aspects of the program and recommendations for improvement. Found to be crucial to the effectiveness of the program were a nonjudgmental attitude, a non-threatening approach, and acceptance of the strengths and vulnerabilities of these relatively independent women. Also essential was an atmosphere that encouraged the women and children to participate without coercion in aspects of the programs according to their needs, interests, and abilities. Specific aspects of the program most appreciated by all were adequate, safe, affordable housing and child care. Other aspects such as parenting groups, the food bank, scholarships for children, support of the staff and board members were meaningful to some but not all, depending on their individual needs. Recommendations included increase in basic income threshold without increasing subsidized rent, more nutritious food and staples in the food bank, timely identification of physical and emotional health problems

---

[38] A confidant was defined as someone readily available with whom a woman could confide personal issues and receive mutual confidences.

[39] Secure attachment pattern was defined by the ability to relate to another person in a trusting, reciprocal, and mutually dependent manner.

[40] An insecure attachment pattern was defined as having either anxious or preoccupied relationships.

and access to appropriate care, improvement in parenting programs to suit the children's ages, development of the transition assistance when families leave the Project Chance program, and obviously increased fund raising for improvement and expansion of the program to include more mothers and their children.

# References

Ainsworth, M., Blehar, M. C., Waters, E., & Wall, S. (1978). *Patterns of Attachment: A Psychological Study of the Strange Situation*. Hillsdale, NJ: Lawrence Erlbaum.

Aisenstein, M. (2012). A particular form of paternal identification in women. *Psychoanalytic Quarterly, 81*: 27–37.

Aisenstein, M. (2015). The question of the father in 2015. *Psychoanalytic Quarterly, 84*: 351–362.

Akhtar, S. (2005). Early relationships and their internalization. In: E. S. Person, A. M. Cooper, & G. O. Gabbard (Eds.), *Textbook of Psychoanalysis* (pp. 39–55). Washington, DC: American Psychiatric Publishing.

Akhtar, S. (2009). *Comprehensive Dictionary of Psychoanalysis*. London: Karnac.

Akhtar, S. (2012). What does a mother do? In: S. Akhtar (Ed.), *The Mother and Her Child* (pp. 1–13). New York: Jason Aronson.

Anderson, M. K. (2019). *From Tribal Division to Welcoming Inclusion: Psychoanalytic Perspectives*. New York: Routledge.

Bacal, H. A., & Newman, K. M. (1990). *Theories of Object Relations: Bridges to Self Psychology*. New York: Columbia University Press.

Balsam, R. H. (2000). The mother within the mother. *Psychoanalytic Quarterly, 38*: 28–51.

Balsam, R. H. (2012). *Women's Bodies in Psychoanalysis.* New York: Routledge.

Balsam, R. H. (2017). Freud, the birthing body, and modern life. *Journal of the American Psychoanalytic Association, 65*: 61–90.

Balsam, R. H., & Harris, A. (2012). Maternal embodiment: A conversation between Rosemary Balsam and Adrienne Harris. *Studies in Gender and Sexuality, 13*: 33–52.

Baraitser, L., & Noack, A. (2007). Mother courage: Reflections on maternal resilience. *British Journal of Psychotherapy, 23*: 171–188.

Benedek, T. (1951). The physiological and psychological aspects of normal pregnancy and childbirth; their significance in illegitimate pregnancy. Proc. 11th Inst. of the Ctee. for the Study of Unmarried Parenthood of the Welfare Council of Metropolitan Chicago.

Benjamin, J. (1991). Father and daughter: Identification with difference—a contribution to gender heterodoxy. *Psychoanalytic Dialogues, 3*: 277–299.

Benjamin, J. (1995). *Like Subjects, Love Objects.* New Haven, CT: Yale University Press.

Bishop-Gwyn, C. (2019). *Art and Rivalry: The Marriage of Mary and Christopher Pratt.* Toronto, Canada: Alfred A. Knopf Canada.

Bowlby, J. (1988). *A Secure Base: Parent–Child Attachment and Healthy Human Development.* New York: Basic Books.

Britton, R. (1989). The missing link: Parental sexuality in the Oedipus complex. In: J. Steiner (Ed.), *The Oedipus Complex Today* (pp. 83–101). London: Karnac.

Brockes, E. (2018). *An Excellent Choice: Panic and Joy on My Solo Path to Motherhood.* New York: Penguin.

Chodorow, N. (2000). *Reflections on the Reproduction of Mothering—Twenty Years Later. Studies in Gender and Sexuality, 14*: 337–348.

Churley, M. (2015). *Shameless: The Fight for Adoption Disclosure and the Search for My Son.* Toronto, Canada: Between the Lines.

Clauss-Ehlers, C., Yang Y. T., & Chen, W. J. (2006). Resilience from childhood stressors: The role of cultural resilience, ethnic identity, and gender identity. *Journal of Infant, Child & Adolescent Psychotherapy, 5*: 124–138.

Cobb, S. (1976). Social support as a moderator of life stress. *Psychosomatic Medicine, 38*: 300–314.

Desmond, M. (2020, May 10). *Evicted: Poverty and Profit in the American City.* New York: Crown, Penguin Random House. *New York Times*, Book Review, p. 10.

Diamond, M. J. (1998). Fathers with sons: Psychoanalytic perspectives on "good enough" fathering throughout the life cycle. *Gender and Psychoanalysis, 3*: 243–299.

Easser, R. B. (1974). Changing concepts of the psychology of women: A reconsideration of female sexual development and the role of women. Presented to the Canadian Psychoanalytic Association, June.

Eisold, B. K. (2005). Notes on lifelong resilience: Perceptual and personality factors implicit in the creation of a particular adaptive style. *Psychoanalytic Psychology, 22*: 411–425.

Fairbairn, W. R. D. (1954). *An Object Relations Theory of the Personality.* New York: Basic Books.

Fallon, A. E., & Brabender, V. M. (2012). *A Secure Connection.* In: S. Akhtar (Ed.), *The Mother and Her Child* (pp. 15–43). New York: Jason Aronson.

Fessler, A. (2006). *The Girls Who Went Away.* New York: Penguin.

Fine, S. (2021, June 26). Justice. *Globe and Mail.*

Finley, D. (2020). *The Lost Twin.* London: HQ/HarperCollins.

Fonagy, P., Steele, M., Steele, H., Moran, G. S., & Higgitt, A. C. (1991). The capacity for understanding mental states: The reflective self in parent and child and its significance for security of attachment. *Infant Mental Health Journal, 12*(3): 201–218.

Freeman, T. (2008). Psychoanalytic concepts of fatherhood: Patriarchal paradoxes and the presence of an absent authority. *Studies in Gender and Sexuality, 9*(2): 113–139.

Freud, S. (1912c). Types of onset of neurosis. *S. E., 12*: 227–238. London: Hogarth.

Freud, S. (1923b). *The Ego and the Id. S. E., 19*: 3–63. London: Hogarth.

Freud, S. (1924d). The dissolution of the Oedipus complex. *S. E., 19*: 171–180. London: Hogarth.

Freud, S. (1940a). *An Outline of Psycho-Analysis. S. E., 23*: 139–206. London: Hogarth.

Freud, Sophie (1991). *My Three Mothers and Other Passions.* New York: New York University Press.

Furman, E. (2001). *On Being and Having a Mother.* Madison, CT: International Universities Press.

Garmezy, N. (1993). Children in poverty: Resilience despite risk. *Psychiatry, 56*: 127–136.

Gedo, J. E. (1965). Unmarried motherhood: A paradigmatic single case study. *International Journal of Psychoanalysis, 46*: 352–357.

Gibb, C. (2015). *This Is Happy*. Toronto, Canada: Doubleday.

Glaser, G. (2021). *American Baby: A Mother, a Child and the Shadow History of Adoption*. New York: Viking. *Globe and Mail*, Editorial, July 17, 2019.

Goulding, J. (1998). *The Light in the Window*. London: Poolbeg/Random House.

Harari, Y. N. (2011). *Sapiens: A Brief History of Humankind*. [Translated from Hebrew.] Toronto, Canada: McClelland & Stewart, 2014.

Harris, A. (2008). "Fathers" and "Daughters". *Psychoanalytic Inquiry, 28*: 39–59.

Hawthorne, N. (1850). *The Scarlet Letter*. London: Legend Classics, 2020.

Heti, S. (2019). *Motherhood*. London: Harvill Secker.

Hobson, L. Z. (1970). *The Tenth Month*. New York: Dell.

Jacobson, E. (1968). On the development of the girl's wish for a child. *Psychoanalytic Quarterly, 37*: 523–538.

Knott, S. (2019). *Mother: An Unconventional History*. London: Viking.

Kulish, N., & Holtzman, D. (1998). Persephone, the loss of virginity and the female oedipal complex. *International Journal of Psychoanalysis, 79*: 57–71.

Land, S. (2019). *Maid*. New York: Hachette.

Liebman, S., & Abell, S. (2000). The forgotten parent no more: A psychoanalytic reconsideration of fatherhood. *Psychoanalytic Psychology, 17*: 88–105.

Luthar, S. S., & Barkin, S. H. (2012). Are affluent youth truly "at risk"? Vulnerability and resilience across three diverse samples. *Development and Psychopathology, 24*: 429–449.

Luthar, S. S., Cicchetti, D., & Becker, B. (2000). The construct of resilience: A critical evaluation and guidelines for future work. *Child Development, 71*: 543–562.

Luthar, S. S., & Ciciolla, L. (2015). Who mothers mommy? Factors that contribute to mothers' well-being. *Developmental Psychology, 51*: 1812–1823.

MacDonald, N. (2019, May 22). From the streets to the halls of justice: Former foster child, teen mom overcomes adversity to graduate in law. *Globe and Mail*.

Main, M. (1993). Discourse, prediction and recent studies in attachment: Implications for psychoanalysis. *Journal of the American Psychoanalytic Association, 41S*: 209–244.

Masten, A. S. (2001). Ordinary magic: Resilience processes in development. *American Psychologist, 56*: 227–238.

Mayer, E. L. (1985). Everybody must be just like me: Observations on female castration anxiety. *International Journal of Psychoanalysis, 66*: 331–347.

McCourt, F. (1996). *Angela's Ashes*. New York: Charles Scribner's Sons.

McLachlin, B. (2019). *Truth Be Told: My Journey through Life and the Law*. Toronto, Canada: Simon & Schuster.

National Association of Social Work. There are a number of articles and books about mother and baby homes in the US listed on the website (last accessed 2021).

Notman, M. T., & Nadelson, C. C. (1993). Reproductive choices and development: Psychodynamic and psychoanalytic perspectives. In: D. E. Stewart & N. L. Stotland (Eds.), *Psychological Aspects of Women's Health Care* (pp. 341–349). Washington, DC: American Psychiatric Press.

O'Neil, M. K. (2004). *The Unsung Psychoanalyst: The Quiet Influence of Ruth Easser*. Toronto, Canada: University of Toronto Press.

O'Neil, M. K. (2015). The hopelessness, helplessness dyad: A concluding commentary. In: S. Akhtar & M. K. O'Neil (Eds.), *Hopelessness: Developmental, Cultural, and Clinical Realms* (pp. 203–214). London: Karnac.

O'Neil, M. K. (2016). Single mothers and women's autonomy. In: S. Akhtar (Ed.), *The New Motherhoods: Patterns of Early Child Care in Contemporary Culture* (pp. 51–66). Lanham, MD: Rowman & Littlefield.

O'Neil, M. K., Capel, T., & Hachey, L. (2008). *Program Outcome Study: Contributors to Mother Child Development*. Residence Project Chance Inc., Montreal, Canada: Report to Fondation Lucie et André Chagnon.

Panksepp, J., & Biven, L. (2012). *The Archeology of Mind: Neuroevolutionary Origins of Human Emotions*. New York: W. W. Norton.

Petrie, A. (2013). *Gone to an Aunt's: Remembering Canadian Homes for Unwed Mothers*. Toronto, Canada: McClelland & Stewart.

Pfuhl, E. H. (1978). The unwed father: A non-deviant rule breaker. *Sociological Quarterly, 19*: 113–128.

Picard, A. (2019, July 16). Our history with the abortion pill is shameful. *Globe and Mail* Opinion.

Rabideau, T. (2019, December 29). As the ball dropped, our life fell apart. *The New York Times*.

Rich, A. (1976). *Of Woman Born: Motherhood as Experience and Institution*. New York: W. W. Norton, 1995.

Rutter, M. (1987). Psychosocial resilience and protective mechanisms. *American Journal of Orthopsychiatry, 57*: 316–331.

Rutter, M. (2006). The promotion of resilience in the face of adversity. In: A. Clarke-Stewart & J. Dunn (Eds.), *The Jacobs Foundation Series on*

*Adolescence. Families Count: Effects on Child and Adolescent Development* (pp. 26–52). Boston, MA: Cambridge University Press.

Rutter, M. (2012). Resilience as a dynamic concept. *Development and Psychopathology, 24* (Special Section): 335–344.

Sandler, J., & Sandler, A.-M. (1998). *Internal Objects Revisited.* London: Karnac.

Sandler, L. (2020). *This Is All I Got.* New York: Random House.

Scharff, J. S. (1994). *The Autonomous Self: The Work of John D. Sutherland.* Northvale, NJ: Jason Aronson.

Schneller, J. (2021, October 6). Netflix's *Maid* explores the struggles of the have-nots in the U.S. *Globe and Mail.*

Seelig, B., & Rosof, L. (2001). Normal and pathological altruism. *Journal of the American Psychoanalytic Association, 49*: 933–959.

Shean, M. (2015). Current theories relating to resilience and young people: A literature review. Melbourne, Australia: Vic Health, Victorian Health Promotion Foundation.

Sixsmith, M. (2010). *Philomena.* London: Pan.

Spieler, S. (1984). Preoedipal girls need fathers. *Psychoanalytic Review, 71*: 63–80.

Stern, D. N. (1995). *The Motherhood Constellation: A Unified View of Parent–Infant Psychotherapy.* New York: Basic Books.

Stoller, R. (1964). A contribution to the study of gender identity. *International Journal of Psychoanalysis, 45*: 220–226.

Stoller, R. (1968). *Sex and Gender, Volume 1.* New York: Science House.

Stoller, R. (1975). *Sex and Gender, Volume 11.* New York: Jason Aronson.

Stuart, J. (2007). Work and motherhood: Preliminary report of a psychoanalytic study. *Psychoanalytic Quarterly, 76*: 439–485.

Ticho, G. R. (1976). Female autonomy and young adult women. *Journal of the American Psychoanalytic Association, 24S*: 139–155.

Toews, M. (2018). *Women Talking.* Toronto, Canada: Alfred A. Knopf Canada.

Toews, M. (2021). *Fight Night.* Toronto, Canada: Alfred A. Knopf Canada.

Trad, P. V. (1990). On becoming a mother: In the throes of developmental transformations. *Psychoanalytic Psychology, 7*: 341–361.

Trad, P. V. (1991). Adaptation to developmental transformations during the various phases of motherhood. *Journal of the American Academy of Psychoanalysis, 19*: 403–421.

UNESCO (2005). Report: World Conference on Women. Paris: UNESCO.

Ungar, M., Brown, M., Liebenberg, L., Othman, R., Kwong, W. M., Armstrong, M. I., & Gilgun, J. F. (2007). Unique pathways to resilience across cultures. *Adolescence, 42*: 287–310.

Ungar, M. (2008). Resilience across cultures. *British Journal of Social Work, 38*: 218–235.

UNICEF (2006). Annual Report. New York: UNICEF.

Vaillant, G. E. (1992). *Ego Mechanisms of Defense: A Guide for Clinicians and Researchers.* Washington, DC: American Psychiatric Press.

Werner, E. (1989). High-risk children in young adulthood: A longitudinal study from birth to 32 years. *American Journal of Orthopsychiatry, 59*: 72–81.

Werner, E., & Smith, R. S. (1982). *Vulnerable but Invincible: A Longitudinal Study of Resilient Children and Youth.* New York: McGraw-Hill.

Winnicott, D. W. (1957). The mother's contribution to society. In: *The Child and the Family.* London: Tavistock.

Winnicott, D. W. (1960a). The theory of the parent–infant relationship. *International Journal of Psychoanalysis, 41*: 585–595.

Winnicott, D. W. (1960b). Ego distortion in terms of true and false self. In: *The Maturational Processes and the Facilitating Environment: Studies in the Theory of Emotional Development.* (pp. 140–152). New York: International Universities Press.

Winnicott, D. W. (1963). The development of the capacity for concern. In: *The Maturational Processes and the Facilitating Environment: Studies in the Theory of Emotional Development* (pp. 73–82). The International Psycho-Analytical Library, 64: 1–276. London: Hogarth & The Institute of Psycho-Analysis, 1965.

Wright, R. B. (2001). *Clara Callan.* Toronto, Canada: Harper Flamingo Canada.

Young, L. (1954). *Out of Wedlock.* New York: McGraw-Hill.

Young-Bruehl, E. (1990). *Freud on Women: A Reader.* New York: W. W. Norton.

# Index

'This carefully argued and deeply moving book gives a powerful picture of the challenge to women electing to raise a child on their own. Many personal elements in a woman's life make a difference: education, resources, intergenerational support, and, perhaps above all, personal resilience, and psychological strength. Mary Kay O'Neil's work here also makes a clear case for the need for serious and deep social supports. Mothering alone works best in cultures that provide supports in respectful and deeply compassionate ways. This is a book to learn from, whether the reader is a clinician, a teacher, a parent, or a bystander. Mothering alone is daunting work that needs all our support.'

**Adrienne Harris, New York University**

'This excellent book on mothering alone centres on the author's interviews with women from a program that gave single mothers and their children help with lodging and education. The voices of the women shine through and illuminate many facets of the experience: social and economic aspects, family and traumatic issues, resilience, and much else. Skillfully interwoven with these moving comments are examples from clinical practice and literature, and discussions of the biological, psychological, and social aspects of mothering alone. This impressive book has much to offer anyone with professional or other interest in the topic of mothering alone.'

**Joseph Fernando, MPsyc, MD, Director, Toronto Institute
of Psychoanalysis**

'Mary Kay O'Neil, a psychoanalyst with a background in social work and psychology, describes her research in a Canadian programme designed to help those "mothering alone," and combines these research findings with her own deep understanding of psychoanalytic literature, focusing on (amongst other topics) infant and child development, the development of sexuality, the female psyche, the pain(s) and pleasure(s) of pregnancy, childbirth, and of adults remaining together and separating.

'The text is richly illustrated by fictional and factual accounts from literature and film, as well as from her own psychoanalytic clinical practice and her research interviews. Always respectful of the multiplicity of influences which can help or hinder healthy growth, she focuses on what helps, what is needed, what are the factors which can allow a mother to care for her child, to allow them both to flourish. There is hope everywhere in this book, but the hope is not naive or trite, it is a recognition of the powers of resilience, autonomy, and the capacity to care even under extremely difficult circumstances.

'Subtitled "A plea for opportunity," this volume makes a strong case for the importance of attending to both internal and external factors in order to give the best possible hope to mothers, their children, and those who will follow in future generations. This is a thought-provoking, compassionate, and important book which I can unreservedly recommend.'

**Dr Julian Stern, FRCPsych, Consultant Psychiatrist in Psychotherapy,
psychoanalytic psychotherapist, and formerly Director of Adult and Forensic
Services, Tavistock and Portman NHS Foundation Trust, London**

'This important book gives a much-needed voice to the challenges faced by those who "mother alone." Such mothers are often among the most vulnerable or marginalized members of our society. Frequently, they do not have the resources central to nurturing children effectively. Mary Kay O'Neil powerfully illustrates the need for and benefit of providing opportunities for mothers to develop those resources. A mother who takes the opportunity to improve her circumstances will also improve the circumstances of her children, and in doing so will benefit the future of our society. *Mothering Alone: A Plea for Opportunity* should be read widely. It is an important book for those whose work and interests touch on the lives of these families, including those involved in child protection, education, and governance. This book bears witness to the strength of women who parent alone, to their resilience, and to their courage and tenacity in trying to do their best for their families. Society must give these mothers opportunity to achieve that best.'

**Susan E Lang, retired judge of the trial and appellate courts of Ontario**